The Organic Wine Guide

THE ORGANIC WINE GUIDE

Charlotte Mitchell and Ian Wright

MAINSTREAM
PUBLISHING

Copyright © Charlotte Mitchell and Ian Wright, 1987

All rights reserved.
First published in Great Britain in 1987 by
MAINSTREAM PUBLISHING COMPANY (EDINBURGH) LTD
7 Albany Street
Edinburgh EH1 3UG

ISBN 1-85158-075-1 (cloth)
ISBN 1-85158-105-7 (paper)

No part of this book may be reproduced or transmitted in any form or by any other means without the permission in writing from the publisher, except by a reviewer who wishes to quote brief passages in connection with a review written for insertion in a magazine, newspaper or broadcast.

British Library Cataloguing in Publication Data

Mitchell, Charlotte
  The organic wine guide.
  1. Wine and wine making
  I. Title   II. Wright, Ian
  641.2'2   TP546

  ISBN 1-85158-075-1

Typeset in Imprint by Bookworm Typesetting Ltd, Edinburgh
Printed in Great Britain by Billing & Sons Ltd, Worcester

CONTENTS

Foreword	9
Credits	10
Introduction	11
What is Organic Wine?	13
Organic – What Guarantee?	20
How Wine is Made	28
Grape Varieties	31
Labelling	39
Additives and Preservatives in Wine	43
Wine Scandals	49
What Does Organic Wine Cost?	56
France	58
Germany	134
Italy	159
Spain	167
England	170
Switzerland	175
Austria	175
USA	176

Australia	183
Japan	184
Distributors	187
Organic Wine Stockists	190
Food and Wine	195
Glossary	202
Select Bibliography	206
Index	207

For Michael and Jeanie
and in memory of Loek

FOREWORD

I asked Ian Wright to co-write the book because I wanted a wine expert with no organic prejudices to keep an even balance of criticism, so his determination to assess quality and not be swayed by any inclusion or omission of unknown substances has helped to produce a book that is a fusion of two quite different people's views.

My main point is that you should know what you are swallowing – and – with current labelling laws for alcohol you don't, and that you should avoid unnatural chemicals in every area. They are neither good nor necessary for you or the world and you certainly don't need them to make good wine!

We've written to all the organic wine producers that we could find throughout the world – and there are hundreds – and spoken to many despite our doubtful French. The response has been better than we had hoped and many have kindly sent samples of their wines for us to write about.

Ten years ago people wanted to know how to cook brown rice (or which one to buy) and for the last couple of years I've been regularly asked of organic wine, "Is it alcoholic?" (Yes – sighs of relief). "Can you drink as much as you like without getting a hangover?" (No – but the effects should be a lot less because of lower sulphur content). Hence this book there wasn't one so we wrote it.

CHARLOTTE MITCHELL
August 1987.

CREDITS

As you can imagine, it's been a lot of fun writing a book about organic wine, although much of the pleasure has been in meeting so many interesting people along the way. We've never had so many exciting letters in our lives as from the wine producers – so a big thank you to everyone who has sent us samples and information, producers and importers.

We are indebted to our tasting panel, some of whom have given up much time purely for the pleasure of experiencing so many different wines – Bill Wallace, Grace McCaig, Jim Hogg, John Elvidge, Mike Foulis, Barry Wright, Pete Harvey, Martin Irons, Michael Romer, Nigel McLardie and Paul Sanderson. Thanks also to Mike Foulis and Archie Kyle for their cartography.

Our French has had a good polishing, our German is as bad as when we started, so many thanks to Sylvie Henocque, Catherine Baud and Werner Kittel for their translations, also Olga Amadei for help with Italian and Pete Harvey with Dutch. Thanks also to Julie Paul, Nicola Smith and Heather Thomson for their secretarial skills.

The book is dedicated to Loek uit het Broek, the man who went to teach the Third World how to farm with chemicals and came back to teach the West how not to, and without whose help this book would not have been written. He died in an accident on Easter Saturday 1987, and the world is a poorer place without him.

Finally a big thank you to Michael Grimm Foxen for love and reason and to Jeanie Wright for her support.

INTRODUCTION

It seems to have escaped the attention of the wine industry that food manufacturers have scored a huge success as a result of their new policy of leaving out the additives that were required to be put on the label by recent EEC law; the public have been proven to be more discerning than originally thought. Recent scandals about the adulteration of wine have brought home the fact that it is not just the unscrupulous few who fiddle but that it is the general practice to "improve" what should be a clean natural product.

The marketing people may throw up their hands in horror at the idea of naming all ingredients on a label but the current position in the United States is that we are likely to see further elaboration on the Federal Law requiring all sulphites to be stated on the label, as is the case in Australia. Although the official line of the British Ministry of Agriculture is that they do not support ingredient labelling for alcoholic drinks within the EEC, public pressure backed by the Consumer Association (and hopefully by this book) will make this information on a label inevitable. Why don't we do something positive about it now?

There is constant attention in the media to the catastrophic damage being done to the environment by the short-sighted use of chemicals and the physical destruction of such as the rain forests. This attention gives increased impetus to the argument for a more reasoned ecological approach to the food and drink supply, making organic agronomy an obvious approach to the future. As part of this we feel there is a need to bring to a larger public the great number of wines being made by a careful and caring group of people who not only grow the grapes but make their wines

THE ORGANIC WINE GUIDE

without recourse to the chemicals and additives which we could do without.

In this, the first *Organic Wine Guide*, we have listed all the wines known to us although some may not be immediately available in the UK. There is a growing number of wholesale and retail outlets, listed in the guide, and many people have access to overseas outlets.

Tastings were carried out over a period of months and involved both enthusiastic amateurs and people from the trade in an attempt to achieve both informed and unbiased opinions on the wines in question. The tasting notes accompanying the entries in the book are a summary of the results. The layout of the entries is basically by country, region and wine label. In France the predominant name on the label has been used and in Germany the area/vineyard name has been used, e.g. Bahlinger Silberberg (area/vineyard) and subfiled by producer. We have tried to give background information and tasting notes on as many wines as possible but because this is the first *Organic Wine Guide* we decided to list those we do not know too much about on the grounds that the reader may want to know they exist and perhaps to try them. Where a producer has more than one entry we have not duplicated the background information and there is an index to pinpoint any particular wine in which the reader is interested.

You pay more for organic wine at the bottom end of the market than you would for an ordinary vin de pays, but then you are not getting something that has been mass produced. Because of the more personal attention organic wine production requires it can create more individual character in the wine. One rarely encounters the blandness found in larger commercial blends. Organic vinification does not allow a poor wine to be disguised so you can also discover the occasional horror.

Many of the wines tasted and the wines available in Britain tend to be young. This is not because they are incapable of ageing but because the makers, mostly small concerns, may not be able to tie up capital in the product before releasing it on to the market. But a lightly sulphured, hand-made wine is more likely to turn into something interesting than some pasteurised bottle from the supermarket shelf.

WHAT IS ORGANIC WINE?

A surprisingly large number of people, including in some instances wine professionals, are unclear as to whether organic wines are alcoholic or have anything to do with grapes. A spokesman for the Wine and Spirit Association in London recently announced in strongly worded terms that there is no such thing! The misapprehension stems from the idea that if it's good for you it's suspicious, if it's healthy or different it must be cranky; nothing could be further from the fact. Organic as a term describes a method of agriculture that has centuries of history as its pedigree and a commonsense, realistic attitude to the future as its aim. Wine is just wine – fermented alcoholic grape juice.

Organic wine makers use traditional methods with prohibitions on a whole range of harmful modern chemicals and physical methods used by commercial producers to improve quality and mask bad characteristics. Today's wine "factories", some of which look more like a nuclear reprocessing plant than a sleepy chateau, can input almost anything and the wine always comes out as a standard product. A major advantage of drinking organic wine is that it is not only a natural product but that you can avoid a cocktail of fungicides and pesticides applied to the vines.

Organic agriculture is founded on these basic aims – soil fertility by crop rotation and feeding with natural substances and biological rather than chemical pest and weed control. It is backed by ethically sound principles, to produce high-quality food without damage to the environment present *or* future, is sustainable and promotes a healthy diet not only for humans but also animals, in particular livestock.

The organic farmer uses biological (natural) techniques for pest control, for instance introducing insects to feed on other insect pests to maintain a balance, and also disease control by introducing organic substances from pectin to shrimp shells, to inhibit problems such as fungi, bacteria or viruses from developing. Many conventional farmers are adopting biological methods in the growing knowledge that pests are rapidly showing resistance to chemical pesticides and that with chemical control the problems are sometimes getting worse, not better.

One may wonder where a large-scale commercial farmer gets enough ladybirds, earthworms or hedgehogs to enable him to use biological pest control methods. This problem has in fact been tackled by very sophisticated methods, for instance a factory, "The Sterile Screw-Worm Fly Production Plant", exists in Mission, Texas, and round-the-clock shifts produce 170 million sterile flies a week! Elaborate precautions have to be taken to ensure no fertile flies escape and turn into predators. All staff have to strip, wash and re-dress in clean clothing on each exit and entry to the factory. Around 25,000 gallons of water are used along with over 700 tonnes of food (a day) to feed the flies (screw-worm is a pest severely affecting cattle, sheep and goats in America, the Caribbean and Mexico). So this is no half-baked operation.

Chemical pesticides are also extremely expensive. One area where organic agriculture definitely scores is that it is obviously cheaper to do without, though the organic viticulturist produces less grapes per hectare than the conventional grape-growing wine-maker, as one would expect.

The vicious circle of chemical pesticide spraying has seriously affected some wine-makers. In Burgundy the 1980 vintage was saved from rot fungi by chemical pesticide spraying. However, the 1983 vintage, an outstanding one, was for many a failure as the grapes succumbed to rot, their skins having been weakened by overspraying, thus rendering them more susceptible to fungal problems at the same time as the fungi had become more resistant.

Organic farming also concentrates most importantly on soil

fertility, the decline of which is a major problem for food production today. The aim is to feed the soil so that the plant can most effectively feed itself. Soil management is fundamental to successful organic farming, the goal being optimum soil structure and fertility. The land is treated (in more ways than one!) to applications of compost, manure and mineral fertilisers (such as rock phosphate, limestone, seaweed and chalk). Green manure crops such as clover or alfalfa growing alongside the vines are particularly important in organic wine production as vine growing is a monoculture, an inherent problem itself. All farmers know that they cannot successfully plant the same crop on the same field each year, and in organic farming rotation is an important means of minimising weed, pest and disease problems; it is used to build fertility as well as providing the basis of harvesting healthy crops in the longer term. In organic viticulture many farmers grow secondary cash crops, such as strawberries or herbs, to help maintain the balance hard to achieve in a monoculture. Planting between the vines, whether for cropping or green manure, also helps lessen soil erosion and maintains surface moisture, aids water absorption and improves soil aeration.

Soil erosion is an enormous problem in Britain, a conclusion backed by the Government-sponsored survey of England and Wales in 1983, and not just as one naïvely imagines in drought-ridden or monsoon-flooded Third World countries. Alan Gear in the *New Organic Food Guide* states the example of large-scale deforestation (chopping down trees is a major factor in soil erosion) in the Nepalese Himalayas causing such loss of soil that a new island is growing up in the Bay of Bengal which he points out could justifiably be claimed as Nepalese territory!

In Britain today we have a somewhat unbalanced geographical division in our agriculture, with the fertile east of England – dubbed the prairies – put over to enormous fields of cereal and other crops and the wetter, hillier west more predominantly animal-type farming, dairy, beef etc. As so many farmers now specialise in one type of agriculture, they don't have the advantage of mixed farming to provide animal manure for the land and grains and straw for the animals, so they resort to "feeding" the land with chemical fertilisers. On the opposite side of the scale there is such an excess of manure from factory animal farming that it has to be deposited by dumping, and the resultant slurry causes local pollution problems as it is so concentrated, containing chemicals fed to the animals.

It is interesting to note that the largest problem ever to beset wine production was overcome by a biological solution. When, in the Victorian age of open transportation between countries of plants and produce, the American insect *phylloxera* was imported to an unsuspecting Europe, no one anticipated that it would come near to wiping out all European vines. American vines are, for some reason, resistant to *phylloxera*, perhaps through a process of evolution whereby the roots of American vines have developed too tough a skin for the insects to live off. Not so the European vine *(Vitis vinifera)* – its roots have no built-in resistance. Because the aphid attacked the roots of European vines and therefore could not be seen, it took a long time for the cause of dying vines to be discovered. It was first identified in England in 1863, and although the biological solution of grafting was first mooted in 1869, it was not until 1874 that it was first seriously approached. Maybe it was the blinding beauty of such a simple solution that threw a scared public off the scent. The French Government had complicated matters by offering a prize of 300,000 francs to the person who could find a solution to the disaster and many were proffered – from burying a live toad in a container to extract the poison (a solution also found in Pliny's *Natural History*) to flooding the vineyards with an explosive mixture of water and carbon bisulphide. How many accidents were caused in the widespread testing of this latter theory one can only wonder at.

In fact, the first biological solution examined was to replant Europe's vineyards with American grapes, and producers were horrified at the thought of the foxy-tasting wine that that would produce. Grafting on to American roots solved this problem, and from 1880 to 1890 over 1,400 hectares of vineyards were replanted. This practice still goes on, using more sophisticated methods of grafting, and the beauty of it is that it is a once-and-for-all process, unlike chemical pesticide treatment

WHAT IS ORGANIC WINE?

which not only has to be carried out regularly, but at great recurring expense.

So the basic theory behind organic agriculture and viticulture is soil fertility, crop rotation and biological pest control. The commercial farmer, aware of his soil erosion, pollution and expensive fertilisers, in many cases would love to turn to organic agriculture, but is most frequently heard to say he cannot risk it – what would happen if all his crops were wiped out? The awful truth is, however, becoming apparent – can he afford not to? How long will the taxpayer be prepared to support an ecologically damaging, outrageously expensive industry that is in any case on a treadmill of using so many chemicals that the choice of seed is narrowing fast to a few resistant varieties? What if, with continued use of pesticides, his choice becomes wiped out? Many people are desperately worried about the lack of varieties of cereals, vegetables and fruit, and not only from the resistance point of view. EEC regulations are interpreted so strictly in the UK that produce must also be of standard size, colour and shape. The consumer will have noticed the lack of choice in vegetable types in the last decade in the UK, unlike in France, for instance, where they put a different, more commonsense, interpretation to the rules. There are too few seed banks where the unused and unusual seeds are stored, and if any accident befell them we would have lost our legacy of choice and variety – whether we ever manage to utilise it anyway is another matter.

There may also become such severe health constraints on use of chemical agriculture that alternatives will be forced on the farmer. Rachel Carson, whose book *Silent Spring* first sounded the alarm, stated: "What we have to face is not an occasional dose of poison which has accidentally got into some article of food, but a persistent and continuous poisoning of the whole human environment!"

Perhaps people feel blasé about the loss of wildlife or plant varieties, so what will it take to make them exert pressure for change in our environment – the death of a baby or a friend? Stanley Clinton Davies, the EEC Environment Commissioner, has threatened this August 1987 to take the British Government to the European Court in Strasbourg for failing to meet or

THE ORGANIC WINE GUIDE

satisfy health standards in British water, a fundamental necessity for living if ever there was one. It's not so easy however – one can't just change the mixture in the taps.

It is an undisputed fact that over 50 water authorities in the UK have nitrate levels in their water over the 50mg per litre safety limit set by the EEC – so our Government gives them a new ceiling of 80mg! And East Anglia has something verging over 150mg! This problem is partly the result of nitrates that have taken years – perhaps 15 to 20 – to soak through our soil into the underground water system, and thus to our reservoirs and our taps. What will happen in 20 years' time when today's increased nitrate levels from chemical agriculture appear in our drinking water? Already some water authorities provide bottled water for lactating mothers as nitrate is stored in the body's fat layers and breast-feeding will release it in concentrated form into breast milk. (One reason why it may also be dangerous to go on a diet with fast weight, or fat, loss, and also a reason why testing noxious chemicals on caged rats or other animals may not show up the true potential for damage of a drug. The animals do not use up fat, and therefore the chemical, in the same way as they would if running wild, so clinical testing by these methods may be unreliable. The public has already been made aware of the ravages of "safely" tested drugs on the human race.)

Perhaps all this is an argument for laying down water as well as wine. The nitrate levels in water cause miscarriage, blue babies, stomach and other cancers, and it must be emphasised that although it is highlighted here, nitrate is by no means the only chemical in our water supply above safety limits. The United States National Academy of Sciences (USNAS) states that the three pesticides, dieldrin, endrin and aldrin, known collectively as the drins, "present the greatest hazard of all residual pesticides in water". And it has been shown recently that the UK has relaxed permitted safety limits sixfold to allow existing levels of these pollutants to continue. The USNAS goes on to state: "At low dosages, they are highly active heptacarcinogens (causes of liver cancer) and have a dangerous effect on the central nervous system of man and higher animals, leading to apparently irreversible encephalographic and

WHAT IS ORGANIC WINE?

behavioral patterns". Half of England is affected by this problem, despite Government assurances that standards of pesticides in water and other areas would be based on "sound scientific judgement"!

One of our eminent wine tasters for this book, Jim Hogg of J E Hogg Wines, Cumberland Street in Edinburgh, states that when tasting wine, his cut-off point for quality comes when he would prefer to drink a glass of water – I hope this wise maxim is not going to have to be washed down the plug hole.

Although we call our planet "Earth", less than 10% of the surface is tilled by the plough. On that surface in 1985 we dumped 2,300 million kilos of pesticides, and presumably even more in 1986. This equals about half a kilo per annum for every human being in existence!

We would not argue that turning to organic wine is a worthwhile thing to do on an organic basis alone if it were not that the wines produced by this well-thought-out, careful method were not such splendid alternatives. Obviously, as in all production, there are those that do not turn out well, and without chemicals to disguise this fact they may perhaps be very basic unpretentious drinking. But the true wine-lover stands to be thrilled and excited by some of the wines that are made. Their clarity and vitality is more obvious than some commercial wines, their quality in many examples truly great.

ORGANIC – WHAT GUARANTEE?

Inevitable confusion over the exact meaning of the term "organic" has arisen, and naturally the public wants to know what guarantees they have that the wine has indeed been produced without artificial additives, pesticides, fungicides or fertilisers. Not all organic wines at the moment carry one of the certification symbols, and some producers, refuse to use them on the basis that they are not strict enough in their qualifying standards.

But organic – what does it mean? In France and Germany the term "biological" is used, all too confusingly connected in the United Kingdom with clothes washing powders of a very chemical make-up indeed! The dictionary definition of organic indicates that it means a class of compounds which naturally exist, a substance or living thing formed (or organised) from living or natural constituents. Does this, then, mean only a product which has not been tampered with in any way, or one to which nothing has naturally grown?

For our purposes here we attempt to clarify the term "organic'" as used in today's food and drink market, because although it could well be construed not to be at all the correct description, it is the one in common usage, and is generally understood and accepted to be the description for chemical-free products of an agricultural system without artificial inputs. The use of the word in the wine trade has produced more argument and confusion than in the natural food world, because wine has traditionally required certain treatments, notably the use of sulphur for sterilisation, which one could conclude renders the term "organic" totally inappropriate.

ORGANIC – WHAT GUARANTEE?

One Edinburgh wine merchant argues that many of the great wines are made organically anyway, and therefore the present interest in organic wine looks rather like a marketing hype. Purists will no doubt be upset by the fact that some producers are now keen to farm and vinify organically because they see that it will increase sales but, whatever the reason, surely this is great news – a breakthrough? It is no longer the situation of the committed few caring wine producers battling against a world covered in tons of chemicals. (Where do they all go?) On the contrary, it is becoming good commercial practice, and those who have worked so hard for ideological reasons may hopefully see some profit for their efforts in the future.

This is where the system of certification comes in, a standard which is recognisable by a symbol or name which the consumer can trust, and can refer to in the rules for growing and production. It would be interesting to compare the growing methods of the great names involved in chemical-free production, because many would argue it is not only what you put in your wine but, more importantly, how you grow your grapes. One has got to look at organic agriculture in general to understand what is happening.

If you do decide to take this road, there are several organisations who will not only certify your farm and produce as meeting their defined organic standards but who will provide detailed guidelines and recommendations on such agricultural methods. As organic farming has been the norm for most of history it has now reached very sophisticated heights. It is not just a question of leave out the chemicals and add a few predatory bugs! The regulatory organisations provide detailed directives for all aspects of farming and its inherent problems, as well as, in the case of wine, vinification. They require their members to sign agreements, keep documentary records, and to follow their principles.

We produce here two examples, signed by Noël Michelin (who produces the Terre Blanche wines from Provence available in the UK) of an agreement with the Fédération Européenne des Syndicats d'Agrobiologistes whose membership logo is "Terre et Vie" (Land and Life). Also a Le Maire Boucher contract with Jean-Claude and Annie Loupia.

THE ORGANIC WINE GUIDE

ENGAGEMENT QUALITATIF

Production de l'Agriculture Biologique

Garantie "TERRE ET VIE"

| CONTRAT N° |

NOM : ...Michelin...
PRENOM : ....Noël.........
Adresse : ...Domaine des Terres Blanches 13210 St Remy de Provence
Tél : 90.95.91.66

ARTICLE 1 - ENGAGEMENT

L'agrobiologiste-souscripteur :
- atteste de son droit à l'exploitation de la Surface Agricole Utile (S.A.U.) décrite ci-après ;
- s'engage à respecter les clauses du cahier des charges de la F.E.S.A dont il déclare avoir pris connaissance ;
- accepte l'accès en tous lieux de son exploitation sans formalité, ni avertissement préalables à toutes personnes mandatées par la F.E.S.A. pour le contrôle du présent engagement ;
- déclare être adhérent au Syndicat des Agrobiologistes de son département, membre de la F.E.S.A.

ARTICLE 2 - UTILISATION DE LA GARANTIE "TERRE ET VIE"

En contre-partie de l'engagement précité, l'agrobiologiste-souscripteur est autorisé à se prévaloir de la <u>garantie "TERRE ET VIE"</u> pour les productions issues des parcelles de son domaine reconverties à l'agriculture biologique depuis deux ans.

Il est interdit de cultiver la même année une même variété à la fois sur des parcelles en agriculture biologique en reconversion biologique, et en "agriculture classique". Il en va de même pour les races d'animaux.

ARTICLE 3 - DUREE DE L'ENGAGEMENT, PROROGATIONS ANNUELLES ANNULATIONS, CAS DE FORCE MAJEURE

L'utilisation de la garantie "TERRE ET VIE" est accordée jusqu'au 31 décembre de l'année de la signature de l'engagement.

L'autorisation pourra être prorogée par la signature d'un avenant annuel au présent engagement, l'absence de renouvellement entraînant automatiquement l'annulation de l'autorisation.

./...
(Suite page 4)

ORGANIC – WHAT GUARANTEE?

DECLARATIO

PRODUCTION

En Agriculture ~~classique~~ Biologique
depuis la création du domaine : 1968

Nom des Parcelles	Numéro de Cadastre	Surface	CULTURES DE L'ANNEE espèce - variété VIGNE
	HT 06	12ha 06	2 ha 83 — grenache
	"		3 ha 07 — grenache
	"		3 ha 08 — grenache
	"		1 ha 54 — Cabernet-Sauvignon
	"		1 ha 54 — Cabernet-Sauvignon
	HT 07	24ha 19	1 ha 37 — Cabernet-Sauvignon
	"		1 ha 30 — Syrah
	"		2 ha 33.10 — Syrah
	"		2 ha 20 — Mourvèdre
	"		1 ha 37 — Mourvèdre
	"		0 ha 82.50 — Mourvèdre
	"		4 ha 40 — Cinsault
	"		2 ha 20 — Counoise

PRODUCTIO

ESPECE	RACE	NOMBRE

THE ORGANIC WINE GUIDE

S.A.U. Totale : ......4.0. HA

DE SURFACES

dont S.A.U. en AGRICULTURE BIOLOGIQUE :
...3.8.. HA 86a 22c

VEGETALES

En Agriculture Biologique, suite

Nom des Parcelles	Numéro de Cadastre	Surface	Date du Début de la reconversion à la création : 1968	CULTURES DE L'ANNEE espèce - variété
	HT07		4 ha	Ugni Blanc
	"		0 ha 30	Clairette
	" dont	3ha 89.40	en jachère avant replantation hiver 87	
	HT09	2ha 50.62	0 ha 82.62	Sauvignon Blanc
	"		1 ha. 68	Cabernet-Sauvignon
	Total	38ha 86.22	38ha 86.22	

S ANIMALES

ESPECE	RACE	NOMBRE

ORGANIC – WHAT GUARANTEE?

Si pour une raison indépendante de sa volonté, le souscripteur se trouve empêché de respecter l'un des aspects de son engagement, il doit pour dégager sa responsabilité, en avertir sa clientèle, son Syndicat départemental et la F.E.S.A., par lettre recommandée ; l'autorisation sera suspendue jusqu'à nouvel avis des responsables syndicaux.

En cas d'apport de nouvelles parcelles (échanges de terres, agrandissement) l'agrobiologiste-souscripteur devra en avertir, sous 48 heures, son Syndicat départemental et la F.E.S.A.

ARTICLE 4 - ETIQUETAGE

La marque déposée "TERRE ET VIE" ne pourra être utilisée pour l'étiquetage sans l'accord préalable de la F.E.S.A.

L'étiquetage devra en outre être conforme à la législation en vigueur concernant le conditionnement et l'étiquetage, mais également à la législation sur l'Agriculture biologique (loi d'orientation agricole du 4 juillet 1980, décret du 10 mars 1981 sur l'homologation des cahier des charges).

ARTICLE 5 - RESPONSABILITES, SANCTIONS

Le non-respect du présent engagement rend l'agrobiologiste-souscripteur seul responsable vis-à-vis du Service de la Répression des Fraudes et du contrôle de la qualité chargé officiellement de faire respecter la législation en vigueur (Décret du 10 mars 1981 n° 81-271).

En cas de manquement ou tromperie eu égard au présent engagement, l'agrobiologiste-souscripteur encourt le risque de se voir réclamer, par le Syndicat des Agrobiologistes dont il dépend, et par la F.E.S.A., une indemnité à titre de sanction et de réparation de préjudice.

En cas de contestation, seul le Tribunal de Grande Instance d'ANGERS sera compétent.

Fait en 4 exemplaires
à St. Remy de Provence
le 30 mars, 1987

Signature du souscripteur
(précédée de la mention)
"LU ET APPROUVE"

lu et approuvé

No**MICHELIN**
TERRES BLANCHES
13210 ST-REMY-DE-PROVENCE
Tél. 90.95.91.66

Le Président
du Syndicat
des agrobiologistes

Le Responsable
de la F.E.S.A.

UNIA - MLB CHAVEIGNES 37120 Richelieu

CONTRAT D'ENGAGEMENT QUALITATIF ANNÉE 1986
N° 86 - 11 - 04 - 017

Production
de l'agriculture biologique
méthode LEMAIRE-BOUCHER
obtenue sans utilisation de
produits chimiques de synthèse
★★★

OU

Production
de l'agriculture biologique
méthode LEMAIRE-BOUCHER
obtenue sans utilisation de
produits chimiques de synthèse
EN RECONVERSION
★ ★

ENTRE :
I. - L'Union Nationale Interprofessionnelle de l'Agrobiologie Méthode Lemaire-Boucher (U.N.I.A.-M.L.B.) ayant son siège à la Mairie de Bourges (Cher),
d'une part,

II. - ET
NOM : LOUPIA Jean Claude et Annie
Prénom :
agriculteur demeurant à :
— lieu-dit : LES ALBARETS
— commune : PENNAUTIER

JEAN-CLAUDE et ANNIE LOUPIA
...
LES ...
11000 ... ...
TE...

UNIA - MLB

UNION NATIONALE INTERPROFESSIONNELLE
DE L'AGROBIOLOGIE METHODE LEMAIRE-BOUCHER

SECRETARIAT : "Aillon"
CHAVEIGNES 37120 RICHELIEU
Tél. (47) 58.22.73

FINANCEMENT DES CONTROLES
Cotisation de Participation
ANNEE 1986

MONSIEUR... LOUPIA Jean Claude et Annie
(Nom Prénom)
Raison Sociale ... Viticulteurs
Adresse ... Les Albarets de Pennautier
... CARCASSONNE .... Tél. 68.24.91.77

Agriculteur, adhérent de l'U.N.I.A. - M.L.B.
Titulaire d'un Contrat Qualitatif
   "Production de l'Agriculture Biologique
   Méthode LEMAIRE BOUCHER"
   ou "Méthode LEMAIRE BOUCHER Reconversion"

S'engage à verser à l'U.N.I.A. - M.L.B. Gestionnaire Responsable du Cahier
des Charges de la "Méthode LEMAIRE BOUCHER", une cotisation de Participation
aux frais de contrôles, destinée au financement :
   - des Honoraires de la SOCOTEC (Société de contrôle
     agissant pour le compte de l'U.N.I.A. - M.L.B.)
   - des analyses accompagnant les contrôles.
   - et de la Promotion de la vente des Productions de la
     Méthode LEMAIRE BOUCHER.

ORGANIC – WHAT GUARANTEE?

In their Cahier des Charges they cover the following subjects: general orientation and objectives of organic agriculture; the principles of following their programme; a definition of chemical and natural substances; methods and conversion times to organic agriculture; the products to choose for this; and recommended materials and detailed facts on physical procedures (for instance sexual traps using synthetic pheronomes to attract male insects, giving also very early identification of the scavengers). Vinification procedures, including sulphur treatment, filtering, clarification and chaptalisation (addition of sugar), are all covered also.

Other organisations also go into detail. Nature et Progrès is the one most commonly found other than Terre et Vie with Le Maire Boucher (who also have much to do with organic wheat production and bread-making) a little less strict in its principles. It uses Terre et Océan as a symbol for farms in conversion to full organic methods. The German symbols are Naturland, Bioland, Demeter (for biodynamic farming), Oinos, Biokreis and Bundesverband Okologischer Weinbau (BOW), in Spain one should look out for the Vida Sana symbol, in Italy, Suole e Salute and for Great Britain you will see the Soil Association symbol.

HOW WINE IS MADE

For an understanding of why something other than grapes goes into wine it is important to have some knowledge of the wine-making process. It must be emphasised that not all additives are necessarily harmful, the trouble being how does one know which additives are in what one is drinking, or which ones are indeed harmful.

The weather and the timing of the harvest determine whether the grapes are fully ripe. If it has been a poor year or the grapes have been picked too early they may be low in sugar, high in acidity and produce thin tart wines, whereas if they have been bombarded with heat they may be too strong and have no balancing acidity.

When the grapes are harvested some get crushed, and because there are yeasts on the skin uncontrolled fermentation may start and speed is therefore essential. The grapes are normally crushed and destalked mechanically and sulphur dioxide is introduced to the juice to kill any wild yeasts and bacteria and prevent spoiling (dried fruits frequently have sulphur dioxide added too as a bleaching agent to lighten the fruit although you can obtain them without in natural food shops). Trouble must be taken not to use too much because it can affect ageing and give a smell, as well as creating health problems. The must (grape juice) is normally checked at this point for sugar content and acidity. If the non-organic wine-maker decides it is too acid he can add calcium carbonate, potassium tartarate or potassium bicarbonate or the commercial preparation Acidex; if it is not acid enough he may add tartaric acid or the juice from green grapes. Sugar too can be added at this stage and this is known as chaptalisation, after

HOW WINE IS MADE

Jean-Antoine Chaptal, the French Minister of the Interior who gave it official sanction in 1801.

Grapes themselves comprise 70%-85% water, 12%-27% sugars (fructose and glucose), 1% acids (tartaric, malic and citric) and approximately 0.1% chemical compounds such as the phenolic compounds which include the pigments (colour) and the tannins (astringency and keeping qualities); most of these latter groups are in the skin, pips and stalks, especially the stalks which are normally removed before fermentation. For red wine the pips and skins are fermented with the must to give colour, tannin and complexity and the wine-maker may draw off the must when he judges enough has been extracted. For white wine only the juice is used although some bigger whites get some skin contact to add character.

Fermentation is started by the introduction of a cultured yeast if the natural yeast on the skin has not been used as would be the practice of organic producers (wine yeast on the skin can tolerate sulphur dioxide). Cultured yeast is the usual practice for commercial wine makers who also use diammonium phosphate or ammonium sulphate to encourage the growth of the yeast. Yeast converts sugar to alcohol but also creates carbon dioxide, esters and heat. Temperature is very important; the lower the temperature the more alcohol and aromatic elements are produced. In making white wine in hot countries cooling systems are used. This helps produce a much more sophisticated product; Italy is a good example of cool fermentation improving quality. With red wines heat is not so critical but if temperatures rise too high the yeast will be killed off and fermentation will cease.

When red wines are fermenting the skins rise to the surface, and to get the benefit of them they must be pressed back into the must manually or by machine or design of vat. When the wine-maker has enough colour and tannin and the must has been drawn off, the skins or pomace are pressed, producing a very dark, tannic liquid which can be added to the fermented must to give even more tannin or it can be fermented into marc. If, as is often the case, the must and skins finish fermenting together the first pressing, called "free run", may be left as it is or again the tannic liquid from the pressing of the skins may be added.

THE ORGANIC WINE GUIDE

When fermentation is finished the must is racked off the lees and may at this stage be fined, using isinglass, gelatin, egg white, casein or bentonite clay or in the case of commercial producers such nasties as potassium ferrocyanide to bring down the suspended material to the bottom of the barrel. The wine may then be filtered through asbestos, porcelain, carbon or cellulose plates, and these can be so fine that nearly all the microbes are removed, thus almost sterilising the wine. The organic wine maker only uses approved natural substances for filtration such as bentonite clay, and occasionally this will result in a slight and harmless sediment in the bottle.

Also after fermentation the "stabilising agents" are added; these include sodium and potassium metabisulphate, sulphurous acid and the crushed geranium-smelling sorbic acid. If the wine is to be bottled quickly diethylpyrocarbonate (DEPC) is sometimes used; this is a substance that is active for 48 hours before breaking down into carbon dioxide and ethanol, which are present in the wine anyway. Inert gas can again be used to avoid contact with the air. Sometimes a second fermentation is encouraged where malic acid is converted into lactic acid (malo-lactic fermentation). This reduces tartness in the wine and increases complexity.

Some wines are made to be drunk when they are fresh and fruity and these are bottled quickly for quick consumption, but some are made to improve by being stored when fruit and tannin come together and subtle changes create something of unguessed-at complexity and flavour. Wines are aged in both cask and bottle, some reaching their peak at two or three years and some at twenty or thirty. Little is known of the ageing process but one element is air. If wine comes into contact with air it oxidises and goes off, this is why at all stages great care has to be taken to keep the two apart; even in the bottle, if the cork fails, the wine can go off. Yet at the same time a very little oxygen improves wine. A great deal of wine is matured in oak casks which impart vanillin and character, while at the same time the wood allows a very little air to be absorbed aiding the maturing process and adds character. However, care is taken to keep the casks topped up to prevent too much air contact. Even when decanted a wine can change character (usually for the better) if allowed time to breathe.

GRAPE VARIETIES

The major element in any wine is, of course, the grape. There are thousands of different varieties and their hybrids and later we list some of the main types under their most commonly known names with some of their synonyms.

Obviously there are a great number of factors which affect the final outcome of the grape such as climate, pests, weather, soil, the skill of the grower and when they are picked but the most important element for flavour is the grape variety. The Chardonnay is the most popular white grape of the moment not only because of its vigour and adaptability but because it nearly always produces wines with a strong aroma and a complex taste. Gewurztraminer, Riesling, Gamay, Pinot Noir and Cabernet Sauvignon are also wines with a flavour of their own.

It must be remembered that most wines are a blend of several grape varieties. Beaujolais and Burgundies are rare in being made from a single grape, Gamay and Pinot Noir respectively. In Bordeaux, for example, Cabernet Sauvignon, Merlot, Cabernet Franc, Petit Verdot and Malbec are grapes that can be blended to make claret. Cabernet Sauvignon provides structure, colour, tannin and longevity, Merlot flesh and alcohol, and Cabernet Franc a spicy complexity.

In Europe the vines used tend to be traditional with the replanting of new, tasty, vigorous, high-yielding varieties a thing of the very recent past; Muller-Thurgau and Kerner are two new white German grapes which are not only used in Europe but New Zealand and South Africa. In the "new world" there is a greater freedom in which vines are planted and also a greater freedom in how they are blended. In Australia grapes grown hundreds of miles apart can be and are brought together in the mixing vat whereas in Europe the locale is all-important.

RED GRAPES

BARBERA
Widely planted throughout the world – for example it provides 12% of California's red wine production – it is most prominent in north-west Italy. It produces a dark fruity wine and its high acidity makes it useful for blending.

CABERNET FRANC
This grape, said to taste of raspberries, violets, olives, pencil shavings and spices, is most famous for its use in making claret; it can account for up to 66% of some Saint Émilions. It is a relative of Cabernet Sauvignon and is generally used to soften that grape's harsher features. Being lighter and less tannic it can be drunk earlier.

CABERNET SAUVIGNON
Used worldwide this is one of the most fashionable red grapes. Growers like it because it is very vigorous, has good resistance to rot and pests and is thick skinned. Wine makers use it because it adds a touch of class, and wine drinkers like it for its flavours of blackcurrant and cedar. In Bordeaux it is the prominent grape in the Medoc and Graves.

CARIGNAN
Grown mainly in France and California this high-yielding grape produces wine with strong colour, extract, tannin and alcohol. In California it is a major ingredient in the so-called "jug wines" and in France it is generally blended with Cinsault and Grenache in Languedoc and Rousillon. Unfortunately it is sensitive to powdery mildew and needs more attention than some others.

GRAPE VARIETIES

CINSAULT
Some people report that this grape can produce wines with a "dog food" aroma but this doesn't stop it from being used in the south of France as a traditional element in the wines of the Languedoc-Rousillon region along with Grenache and Carignan. Not only is it an element in Châteauneuf du Pape but it is used to make rosés, port-type wines and brandy, especially in South Africa. This grape too is sensitive to powdery and downy mildew.

GAMAY
This is the grape that makes Beaujolais. Light purple in colour with an intense fruity aroma, it accounts for 98% of the plantings in the area. Normally considered to produce a wine for scoffing it can produce wines such as Moulin à Vent which can mature up to 10 years and become almost Burgundy-like. The grape doesn't appear to thrive outside the region although some is grown in Touraine and Anjou.

GRENACHE *(Garnacha, Spain)*
Originally a Spanish grape, this tough and high-yielding grape is used for blending. In Spain it is blended with Tempranillo to make Rioja and in France it contributes to the wines of the southern Rhône such as Gigondas, Lirac, Côtes de Ventoux, Côtes du Rhône, Châteauneuf du Pape and Tavel rosé. In Algeria and Morocco it produces reds and rosés, in California rosés and ports, and in Australia it is the second most planted red grape and is blended to produce some of the cheaper wines.

MERLOT
Not the most fashionable of grapes, it is still widely planted and does in fact account for 95% of one of the world's most expensive wines, Château Petrus from the Pomerol area in Bordeaux, and is preferred to Cabernet Sauvignon in Italy. It produces fruity generous wines, blends well with Cabernet Sauvignon maturing relatively quickly.

NEBBIOLO
Nebbiolo is the great grape of the Piedmont in Italy. Concentrated, bitter, alcoholic, dark in colour, it makes wines that mature very well such as Barolo, Barbaresco and Gattinara.

PETIT VERDOT
This grape is used to provide quality, tannin, flavour and sugar, especially in the Medoc. It rarely contributes more than 5% to any blend.

PINOT NOIR
Described by Jancis Robinson as a "minx of a vine", it can produce wine of very varied quality. In Burgundy the wines are very fruity when young but can develop into one of the world's most sophisticated drinks when older even although it is permitted to add sugar to the must (i.e. chaptalisation) before fermentation. It is also used in Champagne and Sancerre rouge but is rarely successful in other parts of the world. It is prone to rot and needs well-drained soils.

SANGIOVESE
An Italian grape with lots of sub-varieties. It makes wines that vary from the very expensive Brunello to nondescript vini da tavola. It is very common in the Chianti region where the younger wine-designers add a touch of Cabernet Sauvignon for oomph and sophistication.

SYRAH *(Shiraz, Australia)*
If you are rich or have been foresighted, think of Hermitage or Côte Rôtie, if not, think of Cornas, St. Joseph, Crozes Hermitage or some of the marvellous Australian wines, and you get an idea of what this grape can do. It is dark, tannic and needs time to mature. In Provence it is used to add character (e.g. Domaine de Trevallon) and in Australia it is both the "work horse" red and the produce of Grange Hermitage which is definitely not a "sweaty saddle" wine. It likes poor soil, is vigorous and is disease-resistant.

GRAPE VARIETIES

TEMPRANILLO
This is used in Rioja where it is blended with Grenache. It bears a resemblance to Pinot Noir and is grown throughout Spain, including Valdepeñas.

ZINFANDEL
Unique to California, the origins of this grape are surrounded in mystery and debate. It is used to make all sorts of wines, from "jug" whites to reds that mature into sophisticated old age. It has a brambly nose, high alcohol, but is sometimes a bit jammy.

WHITE GRAPES

ALIGOTE
Generally considered to take second place to Chardonnay in Burgundy, it can still produce excellent wines. Lighter and more acidic, it makes wines that are best drunk young.

CHARDONNAY
This is perhaps the world's most fashionable white wine grape, producing wines from the sophistication of Chablis and Montrachet to the big, fat, buttery Australians and Californians. It is a tough vine, being able to take cold weather, and the grape can take a bit of ageing in the oak. It is also blended for Champagne.

CHENIN BLANC
One of the flexible grapes, this produces all sorts of wine all over the world. In France it makes such varied wines as Vouvray, Saumur, Côteaux du Layon and Bonnezeaux. In the rest of the world it is used for anything from vins de table to sherries, ports and brandy. When young there is a distinct floral nose (which can be a bit strong) and the acidity can hide the inherent sweetness which needs time to develop.

GEWURZTRAMINER
People use words such as spicy, roses, lychees, heavily scented

and fetid to describe this very distinctive grape. Most famous in Alsace, it is grown throughout Austria, Germany, Italy and the "new world". It can vary in quality but in some years, especially in Alsace, it can mature into something quite unique.

KERNER
One of the new breed of grapes, this is a cross between Trollinger (red) and Riesling (white) which produces wines of good acidity, tasting a little like Riesling and which have the capacity for ageing. It is also a good producer.

MELON DE BOURGOGNE *(Muscadet, Loire; Pinot Blanc, California)*
Best known as the base for Muscadet, this high-yielding grape in that region makes wines that are crisp, fresh, appetising and dry, the traditional accompaniment to seafood. In Burgundy it contributes to Bourgogne Grand Ordinaire and in California it is sometimes aged in oak to make wines somewhat similar to Aligote.

MULLER-THURGAU
The most widely planted grape in Germany, it is also popular in England. It is a relatively modern cross between Riesling and Sylvaner, is low in acid and is the base for the dreaded Liebfraumilch. Very popular in New Zealand where it is usually blended with a little something else to make their medium dry whites.

MUSCAT
Another distinctive grape with as many different varieties as it has names. It is grown all over the world and makes such wines as Moscateo Bianco, Beaumes de Venise, the sweet wines of Samos, Clairette de Die and the liqueur muscats of Australia.

PALOMINO
Low in acid and sugar, this is the grape that is transformed into sherry.

GRAPE VARIETIES

PINOT BLANC *(Weissburgunder, Germany)*
Related to the Pinot Noir, this grape has high acidity and a neutral nose which make it good for blending and is also commonly used as a base for sparkling wines. Popular in both Italy and California, where it is considered to be close to Chardonnay in quality, it is probably most famous in Alsace where it is bottled on its own and blended to make Edelzwicker.

PINOT GRIS *(Tokay d'Alsace, Alsace; Rulander, Germany)*
A mutation of Pinot Noir, this grape produces spicy wines with low acidity, high extract, and which can be similar to white Burgundies. Most common in Germany and Alsace, it also makes fresher wines in Italy and sweet wines in Hungary.

RIESLING
German in origin, this grape produces tart, aromatic, flowery wines with a potential for ageing (e.g. the expensive German Beerenauslesen and Trokenbeerenauslesen). It is a hardy and vigorous grower popular in Alsace, Austria, Italy and the "new world", where it makes dry fruity wines that are chunkier and sometimes aged in oak.

SAUVIGNON BLANC
In Bordeaux it is blended with Semillon to make both dry and sweet wines and on the Loire it is responsible for Sancerre and Pouilly Fumé. It is grown in north-east Italy and California where, incidentally, Robert Mondavi, the famous wine-maker, changed the name of the varietal to Fumé Blanc and thus increased his sales.

SEMILLON
Semillon is grown all over the world and produces wines of varying quality. In Bordeaux it is the major element in Sauterne and Barsac, where its thin skin allows botrytis (noble rot) to develop and in the Hunter Valley of Australia the varietal is of a very high quality indeed.

SILVANER/SYLVANER
This rather neutral grape was one of Germany's most important grape varieties but is now being replaced by newer grapes. It is popular in Alsace where it produces a slightly spicier product.

TREBBIANO *(Ugni Blanc, France)*
Most white wine produced in the world is made from the Trebbiano, largely because of its very high yield. In Italy there are lots of sub-varieties and it is responsible for the likes of Orvieto and Frascati. In the rest of the world, owing to its bland character and high acidity, it is used for blending and for distillation purposes.

VIOGNIER
A rare grape found in the northern Rhône, it produces the unique white wines of Condrieu and Château Grillet.

WELSCHRIESLING
Predominant in middle Europe, this very high-yielding grape makes a range of wines from light and fruity to Trockenbeerenauslesen.

LABELLING

Wine labels tell you only a certain type of information, much of which means little to the uneducated drinker. It is time everybody was put more firmly in the picture and provided with the easily understandable information it is only reasonable to have. Most wine drinkers would agree that the labels on certain bottles of wine are very confusing; you need to be an expert to decipher the information printed on some German labels, never mind the Gothic print that makes reading even the words an uphill battle. German labels give more precise information than any other country, but unless you are in the know much of it means little. The stated grape name may not be recognisable as the equivalent one that you are used to. For instance, what is Pinot Gris in France is called Rulander in Germany and Tokay in Alsace, and the description of whether it is dry or sweet has fooled many an unsuspecting consumer. The house style of wine is very important, and whereas one grower may produce a Kabinett Trocken – kabinett means the minimum must weight (i.e. sugar) should be 73°, more or less depending on region, Trocken means dry – which is dry, another will have stopped his fermentation at an earlier point and have a lower alcohol, but sweeter, wine.

The day when EEC regulations come out forcing all member countries to standardise their information on wine labels is not in sight, but it is worth considering exactly what we do want to know before the decision is forced upon us. One American winery makes their customers think twice; they produce a leaflet which adapts a quote from Saint-Exupéry's *Le Petit*

Prince: "Grown-ups love figures. When you tell them that you have made a friend, they never ask you any questions about essential matters. They never say to you, 'What does his voice sound like? What games does he love best? Does he collect butterflies?' Instead they demand, 'How old is he? How many brothers has he? How much does he weigh? How much money does his father make?' Only from these figures do they think they have learned anything about him." Robert Lindquist, who owns Qupé, the American vineyard in question (and who sports a beard by all accounts), inspires us to ask what we really want to know about our wine. Another American producer, Walter Taylor, the owner of Bully Hill vineyards in upstate New York, not only labels the ingredients in his wines, but on each vintage gives you a potted history of his battle with Coca-Cola who acquired his family vineyards, Taylors. They fired Walter Taylor in 1970 after he made disparaging comments on the quality of product produced by the new owners of the firm founded by his grandfather.

One should beware of any UK wine retailer copying Walter Taylor's idea of listing ingredients unnecessarily. As a marketing ploy it would no doubt be successful at the outset, but without any legal safeguards to check the information it would be too open to abuse and would be the right move in the wrong way. The consumer would stand to get even more confused than he already is about wine ingredients. So to all you budding wine-marketing people reading this, the message is don't steal his thunder.

The Royal College of Physicians may spring a different type of change upon us by using their undoubted force to print health warnings on wine bottles, similar to those already used on cigarette packs. This is not such an outlandish idea as it seems. In their book, *A Great and Growing Evil: The Medical consequences of alcohol abuse*, they underline the dangers of overconsumption, in particular to pregnant women and women in general (the latter being a target market for expansion in the drinks trade). As the Royal College of Physicians have already managed to exert enough influence to help bring about change in tobacco labelling, one can envisage bottles labelled along the lines of: "Government Health Warning: this wine has an alcohol content over 12° and should not be consumed by pregnant women".

The Royal College of Physicians are not the first to feel concerned about the effects of alcohol abuse. Pliny, in his book *Natural History*, warns against a thing that perverts men's minds and produces madness, having caused the commission of thousands of crimes, and being so attractive that "a large part of mankind knows of nothing else worth living for". Even the Old Testament Book of Proverbs (around 500BC) recommends kings not to befuddle their minds but suggests "(give) wine unto them that be of heavy hearts".

In 1970 new food labelling regulations in the UK made manufacturers declare what sorts of additives were being used, for example as preservatives. On 1st January 1986 a new EEC Law came into force requiring manufacturers to state either E numbers or full names of ingredients and the uses to which they would be put (e.g. tartrazine – yellow colouring) other than for flavouring. Not all the ingredients in wine even possess an E number. It is also a requirement to state on food packaging "best before" or "sell by" dates (depending on the time within which they must be consumed). Although this particular regulation would not apply to wine – all products which last over 18 months are exempt – it might be useful knowledge if the best time to drink it were indicated (e.g. Beaujolais: Consume Now) or if there was a recommended length of time to keep it in your cellar before reaching its peak drinkability.

The requirements for labelling a bottle of wine look set for rapid change. In the first place, by May 1989 all bottles will have to state the alcoholic content. This information will be useful not only to those trying to lose weight (regrettably all too often the enthusiastic wine drinker) but also to those trying not to lose their driving licences. If a grape variety is printed on the label of a wine bottle there is no qualification stated for the percentage of that grape used in the wine. Only Austria decrees that when a grape variety is displayed on a label it must be made from 100% of that grape. Within the EEC the rule is that 85% of a particular grape must be used if it is stated. I would personally like to see – apart from a list of ingredients discussed later in Additives – a description of the wine in the opinion of its maker (not God – the vineyard owner). This would perhaps give all sorts of interesting pieces of information as he or she shows preferences, such as food to be eaten with the wine, even temperatures at which the wine should be drunk – a much ignored factor which can make all the difference.

As wine bottles state the year in which they are made, it would be fun for this to be expanded on. It is not necessarily a good year or a bad year for everyone each year – vintages vary geographically and the chronological information might be more relevant if it was qualified by a paragraph on the effects of the weather that year and the results on the quality and price of the wine and size of the harvest. Frey Wines in California attempt this.

Perhaps all this is a tall order, but maybe wine producers will come to see that, like growing organically, interesting information will help sell their wines to a public increasingly curious about what they consume and keen to drink better wine. If nothing else, they could at least tell us if they collect butterflies!

ADDITIVES AND PRESERVATIVES IN WINE

Additives are nothing new. Man has always had a need to preserve his food through the unproductive months of the year and even today traditional preservatives like vinegar, sugar and salt are widely used. In the 20th century we have developed a new conception altogether of additives and preservatives in food and wine: we demand psychological comfort and technical purity; we like our food and drink to be of even colour, texture and quality; and we also like it to have shelf life.

Until cork and glass bottles came into use in the late 17th century preservation of wine rendered a very different product from the drink we are used to today. Early wine using wild grapes probably had honey added to first make the wine, then preserve it, as wild grapes are very high in acid and low in sugar (yeasts make alcohol as a by-product of their reaction with sugar). Alcohol itself acts as a preservative, so much early wine was a strong alcoholic beverage usually watered down when drunk. In Homer's day, around 700BC, the early ancestor of Greek retsina was born by the use of tree resin as a preservative – still allowed in EEC legislation, but only by the Greeks, thank goodness – and Classical Romans are known to have added both salt and spices to preserve their wine. There is a reference around 50BC that Falerian (one of the early Italian wines) was known to improve from keeping; at the same time the first wooden casks are known to have been used by the Romans (earlier wine having been stored in pottery containers) and this ability to limit oxidisation by use of storage in wood has given us our legacy of ageing wine.

Until the 17th century wine would almost certainly not have been kept longer than four or five years, because oxidisation would have turned it to vinegar or at least destroyed flavour and smell. The introduction of corks, which were in use as ale container stoppers at the turn of the 16th to 17th century in England (almost certainly introduced by monks who had visited Spain, the home of the native tree whose bark lining yields the product we know as cork) was a major innovation in wine production.

The English started their tradition as prolific Champagne drinkers earlier than the French with the discovery around 1670 that a sparkling wine resulted from keeping still Champagne wine in corked bottles rather than wooden casks. Slightly sparkling wines had already been produced in casks, a rustic cloudy drink resulting from a second malo-lactic fermentation induced by warm weather in the spring after the vintage, but the introduction of corked bottles provided a much better medium in which to produce a real sparkling wine by the same natural spring-induced fermentation. This very simple method is still unchanged today in the production of certain sparkling wines, the notable organic ones in this book being Blanquette de Limoux from Jean-Claude Beirieu from the Limoux region, and Clairette de Die from Achard-Vincent on the Rhône. In 1670 the French were still using stoppers of hemp soaked in oil, and it wasn't until the turn of the century that the Benedictine monk Dom Pierre Pérignon, who incidentally also discovered the art of using red grapes to make white wine, was the earliest known user of cork stoppers in France. Champagne production is more formalised and sophisticated today, but we've all heard of this early innovator and drunk the legacy of his discoveries!

The other main aid to the preservation of wine was the introduction during the 18th century of glass bottles for storage instead of oak casks, mainly because the art of glass-making had been so refined that slim, storable bottles were made to replace the heavy bulky earlier versions which were not convenient alternatives to wooden casks.

These two innovations, cork and glass, as wine storage implements, have continued virtually unchanged until the

ADDITIVES AND PRESERVATIVES

present, and the luxury of aged wine is one that we have much to rejoice in.

Today the World Health Authority states that over 5,000 compounds are used as additives in food and drinks, and one must not forget the increased use of chemicals in other products – cosmetics, household cleaning aids, medicines and so on. The fashion for blaming ill-health or physical disorders on allergies related to these chemical additives seems well justified. One only has to refer to Adelle Davis's book, *Let's Eat Right to Keep Fit*, and countless subsequent well-researched data on the subject. The maxim that you are what you eat needs to be remembered as we imbibe all manner of unknown substances, because you are what you drink as well! There is increasing worry that two "harmless" ingredients consumed separately may interact to yield a product which is toxic – how is one to know? Do you need a degree in chemistry to feel confident in feeding your family?

Fortunately there is now intense consumer pressure towards additive-free food and drink, and manufacturers can hardly keep up inventing new food products with labels unadorned by E numbers (flavour enhancers, preservatives, colouring and so on). Despite this many additives are still allowed, and used, which cause recognised health problems – for instance tartrazine, a yellow colouring which causes so many problems, especially in children, from respiratory disorders and eczema to hyperactivity, is still widely found. There is a strong case for an update on the list of chemicals allowed in food and drink, certainly to minimise the enormous list and to exclude those known to cause reactions.

A close look should also be taken at additives which find their way into foods but do not need to be listed at all, for instance eggs or fish fingers, true everyday foods. Some factory-farmed eggs contain the aforementioned tartrazine because it is fed to hens to make their egg yolks a deeper yellow, a trick utilised by feed manufacturers to cover up the lack of green foodstuffs fed to hens. One of our local Edinburgh Environmental Health Officers calls this "a gross misrepresentation to get a natural product [an egg] which has a chemical additive in it". The consumer is going to have to get used to pale yolks of varying

THE ORGANIC WINE GUIDE

hues if he eats battery farm eggs without tartrazine. Or better still buy free-range eggs – if the demand is there the supply will grow.

Fish fingers nowadays usually sport labels saying, "Cod fillets, batter and breadcrumbs. No colouring. No flavouring. No preservatives". But, what is in the batter? The above-mentioned contaminated eggs? By law certain additives such as calcium carbonate must be put in white flour (a legacy left over from wartime Britain) and other constituents may be added, for instance bleach. So where are the E numbers on fish finger packets? Hidden? And on wine labels?

Wine today doesn't have to state any ingredients at all on the label in the EEC and the official line from the Ministry of Agriculture (whom we thank for their help) is that Britain is opposed to ingredient labelling for wine. There is obviously, as in the USA, intense industry pressure against such legislation, but this is very short-sighted. Spurious arguments as to the cost of relabelling can be ruled out on the basis that each vintage requires a new label anyway; the fact is that manufacturers and producers feel that if the truth were known a wave of abstinence might flood the profitable consumer market. Why tamper with a successful trade? Much is spent on advertising to enhance the image of wine as the nectar of the gods, produced from sun-ripened grapes in a picturesque vineyard sure to win you success with the woman/father-in-law/beach bum of your choice. You can imagine the new angles advertising agencies would have to come up with: "This wine is as clean as your whiter than white washing – we guarantee never to sell a bottle without potassium metabisulphate."

But surely it is an absurdity that one of the most overabused drugs, alcohol, is exempted from so simple a regulation as ingredient labelling. (It is interesting to note also that the next most abused drug, tobacco, doesn't have ingredient listing either – what's going on?) It is one thing to warn against the dangers of overconsumption of alcohol, but no rein is kept on the overconsumption of chemicals that go along with it. It is all very well to applaud the consumer for his disdain of additive-laden food, but without ingredient labelling on wine he doesn't get the chance to know what he can object to or to choose a bottle with less or no additives.

ADDITIVES AND PRESERVATIVES

The main chemical additive in wine that causes wide problems from headaches and hangovers to allergic reactions is sulphur. One unfortunate German recently died from a reaction to sulphur after drinking a perfectly legal bottle of German wine, and countless asthmatics suffer from varying doses of E220 (sulphur dioxide) in commercial wine. Organic wine-makers certainly don't want to produce vinegar, so sulphur is used to prevent oxidisation, but in a very much more limited capacity (up to the stated levels in their organic standards), way below EEC regulation levels, and generally no more than a one-third maximum quantity. This limitation also helps the taste; in too many commercial wines the nasty sulphur flavour has not been disguised. Although some wine-makers are experimenting with ways to produce their wine without sulphur, it is perhaps more relevant to spotlight the overenthusiastic use in wine production of this chemical and its near relations, potassium bisulphate and potassium metabisulphite. Far too many unthinking producers are too used to tipping it in regardless.

Commercial producers use chemical additives to disguise poorly made wine in a wide variety of ways. In the same way that lead was added to wine to de-acidify it by the Victorians, today a tart flavour is disguised by the addition of calcium carbonate, potassium bicarbonate or potassium tartarate. On the opposite side of the coin additives can be tipped into a wine to give it the acid it lacks to balance the flavour, citric acid, ascorbic acid (vitamin C), potassium sorbate or tartaric acid – the wine-maker can make his choice!

One of the great benefits of growing grapes organically is that the natural yeasts needed for fermentation are present on the grape skins when harvested. The oversprayed commercial grape too often needs a helping cultured yeast to start the process of producing alcohol. Try diammonium phosphate for size.

Organic wines can also at times have a small amount of sediment in the bottle, yet it is strange that this can be thought of as a disadvantage when the vintage port drinker never bats an eyelid or expects anything else. Sediment is filtered out by various natural methods, for instance egg whites, or bentonite

THE ORGANIC WINE GUIDE

(a natural clay substance) in organic wine. Non-organic wine is often clarified by such tasteless little numbers as potassium ferrocyanide (to precipitate particles of copper and iron floating in white wines), dried ox blood powder or sturgeon's air bladders amongst others! The anti-labelling lobby is at pains to point out that none of these wine additives are dangerous – but the USA, unlike the EEC, has banned the potentially lethal (if overused) potassium ferrocyanide.

All to often one reads that additives to wine are not actually harmful – this is uneducated nonsense. Homo sapiens varies enormously – we all have different reactions to different things, witness the unfortunate German asthmatic, so one cannot generalise in this way. And certainly not when with the rogues one turns up in the wine trade it is impossible to know what additives we are so gaily dismissing, or mixing with each other.

Most drinkers seem to know that sugar is added to wine, a process called chaptalisation after the French Agriculture Minister whose bright idea it was. The next bright idea is to get rid of the European wine lake by making it law to use concentrated grape must instead of sugar to increase the alcoholic content of wine; a practice already utilised by the Italians. So although the sugar has been converted by yeast into alcohol one must question the need for this process of adding so much to a wine if it is only to make it several degrees more alcoholic, and perhaps impair the flavour on the way.

The problems of overconsumption of alcohol are widely publicised, and all too commonly painfully felt, whether it is the strong arm of the law or simply the morning-after sensations. What a pity that in an effort to get rid of sugar and grape surpluses we are all educated to shy away from lower alcohol wine.

WINE SCANDALS

It is only the enormous amount of publicity, and the enormity of the deception, that has at last focused public attention on the disastrous results of illegal meddling in the wine manufacturing business. Suddenly the question is on everyone's lips – what does in fact go into a bottle of wine? Many have, with increasing awareness of food additives, been wondering anyway.

In the last decade there has been a great revolution in the eating habits of the British public – more so than any other country in Europe. This is not to be underestimated – it is unusual for such a turnaround to happen in such a basic function as eating other than under unnatural influences, in particular war. Rationing and unavailability of food changed the British public's eating habits, in many opinions to a healthier basic diet in the short term, but in the long term towards a predilection for sweetened, refined foods. Now this has swung back and every supermarket stocks brown rice. When I started selling brown rice at Real Foods in Edinburgh twelve years ago we sold in the region of 50kg a day. Now it's more like 5 tonnes!

The lack of ingredient labelling on wine bottles has kept the consumer in the dark for too long. Now he not only wants to know what he is drinking, but wonders what he might potentially be drinking if the recipe has been fiddled. Wine scandals are not new and neither are potentially lethal additives to alcoholic drinks. Historians now believe that one of the reasons for the decline of the Roman Empire was the adulteration of their wine by lead, albeit unintentionally.

Merchants manufactured a syrup in lead-lined pots which they added to wine as a preservative, so contaminating it. This was compounded by the fact that one of the symptoms of lead poisoning is loss of taste, so even more wine was consumed in an effort to disguise the flavour and get rid of the metallic taste in the mouth. The Victorians, unheeding of history, added lead to tart wines to make them softer and more palatable.

More recently several dozen North American and Canadian beer-drinkers perished after drinking beer laced with a cobalt sulphate foam enhancer, and in Germany a cancer-causing agent – nitrosodimethalmine – was found in some beers. In China in 1985 three men were executed for manufacturing and distributing fake rice wine which was made from industrial alcohol. The lethal doses of methyl alcohol added to Italian wines and the Austrian diethylene glycol horror story of the 1980s have finally made the public sit up and take note.

Almost everyone seems to have heard about the Austrian scandal and the lack of Austrian wines on British shop shelves is proof of its lasting influence, but few know what actually happened or that it had been going on for a decade. The ambivalent drinker may say, "So what's the fuss about, no one is known to have died", but that is naïve. Illegal additives to wine (and beer) have killed people and are dangerous – in a way that we cannot precisely define. More and more health problems are being shown to result from the human body's reaction to unwanted chemicals and even some of the "legal" additives have been demonstrated to cause physical problems and disorders – sulphur in particular.

The initiator of the diethylene glycol scandal was a biochemist employed by a major Austrian wine producer, and therefore in an influential position with great potential to cause damage by tampering with wines. He discovered that diethylene glycol enhanced the sweetness and body of a cheap low-quality wine during his experiments to produce a completely chemical concoction that could pass as real wine. There was only one snag – it costs more than the traditional grape variety to produce. However, he made use of his discovery and even sold the secret to a selected few local Austrian producers.

WINE SCANDALS

One can only presume that they all earned considerable extra profits from this totally illegal practice – until alarm bells first rang in Vienna in December 1974. It would be easy to construe that overgreediness brought about the downfall of the whole masquerade, but it was more probably simple stupidity. A producer attempted to reclaim the VAT paid on a large delivery of diethylene glycol, and his local tax inspector became suspicious. What did he need all that quantity of chemicals for? He investigated what he suspected was a fraud and the whole deception came to light.

At first it appeared as if only a few grammes per litre of the chemical (also used as a constituent of anti-freeze in vehicles) had been used, but later on over 50 grammes per litre were discovered in some wines. The British Industrial Research Association estimated that 35 milligrammes of diethylene glycol in a litre of wine should not harm an average 11-stone male, but this was cold comfort when, in the United States, a citizen died after drinking 70 grammes by mistake. The level of chemical in some wines was obviously potentially deadly. Although there is still much research to be done on this subject, it has been shown that kidney damage occurs when the body has consumed diethylene glycol, through the expulsion of oxalic acid formed in the system.

The Austrian authorities were quick off the mark to alert their German counterparts, but aware of the enormous damage the publicity would cause to the wine trade the Rhineland Palatinate Ministry of Agriculture kept the discovery secret while they tried to find a legal loophole for the German wine producers to sell their wine. The secretary of this organisation was in the end forced to resign over his efforts to subdue the scandal.

By the end of the following year, 1975, nearly five million litres of contaminated wine had been seized. Adverts appeared in German newspapers of the wines to avoid, and later on in the UK. Black (for contaminated) and white (for "legal") wine lists were published, but not before the floor had fallen out of the Austrian wine trade. This was more of a pity for honest producers, for their wine had been gaining in popularity as a comparable alternative to German wines, but a better bargain pricewise. If you can find Austrian wines nowadays the same is certainly true.

The shock waves continued to spread in Germany, and in an attempt to deflect all blame from themselves – as many blended German wines had been found to be contaminated – the Germans had their own wines analysed. The problem was compounded when 65 different wines, supposedly completely from German production, were found to have a diethylene glycol content! This lent weight to the Austrians' refusal in some instances to take the blame and to compensate for their wine exports. They declared it was impossible to determine from where the contamination had come, so . . . had the Germans also been tipping in the illegal sweetener? Or illegally blending their own wine with cheaper Austrian imports? Or were they simply so slap-dash they failed to clean out their storage equipment?

When the dust settled there were many casualties, not least the total Austrian wine export business (Austria's wine trade was in fact halved and one producer has since advertised his wine as "not suitable for use in car radiators"). The Austrian police commissioner investigating the scandal committed suicide from the pressure of work it had generated; many wine merchants went bankrupt or lost enormous amounts of money in unsaleable stocks. In Britain it became an illegal act to offer for sale any Austrian wine not tested for contamination. In Japan for a time they even banned Australian wine in the confusion!

Many wine-lovers were shocked to find some of the great names involved in the scandal – one hopes that lessons have been learned. On a brighter note the local authorities picked up a few hints – they mixed the unsaleable contaminated wine with road salt for use on icy roads and, it was reported, at airports!

Regrettably the diethylene glycol scandal was not confined to Austria and in turn West Germany; Japan in 1985 was badly shaken when the same problem erupted there. One particularly well-known producer was rumoured to have the chemical in a warehouse, but the accusation was never conclusively proved. When the authorities attempted to test suspect wine stocks,

WINE SCANDALS

they had mysteriously been drained from their storage tanks – reportedly an "oversight" by employees. Upon investigation over 90% of the contents of the producer's wine was imported despite being labelled "pure domestic wine", so it was impossible to tell if contamination had been of Japanese origin or not.

The growing domestic Japanese wine trade was badly rocked by the scandal and consumption tumbled. In an attempt to return confidence and order to the disarray the Japanese Government belatedly began to impose labelling regulations, though of a very basic nature. Wine is now required to carry a statement that it has been tested for diethylene glycol contamination, but amazingly enough only imported wine! As it had been fully proved that dishonest blending and labelling was going on this decision can only be wondered at – why not include domestic product and restore credibility?

ITALY AND METHYL ALCOHOL

Italy has never looked back from its first great vintage, in 121 BC, when it overtook Greece in the popularity of its wines and in modern production methods; she could produce over 1,600 gallons per acre, far more than the traditional Greek producers.

Much has changed since the time when the finest vintages were kept until they were as rich and sticky as honey, to be watered when drunk. There have been problems along the way, notably the lead poisoning mentioned earlier in this chapter, but Italy is now the world's largest wine producer in terms of volume output, although Russia may soon have the largest acreage of vineyards in the world. Employing 7.5% of the population Italy manufactures in the region of 1,700 million gallons per annum, around one-third of which is exported, mainly as a cheap and strong ingredient to blend or be sold at low prices. Sadly, too many of us view Italian wine as something in a carafe in cheap restaurants or in supermarkets; perhaps this is good news – many superb wines, organic and commercial, await those willing to delve deeper into the wonderful range of wines available.

The long history of Italian wine, though, has been dealt a

massive blow by the uncovering in 1986 of a scandal of wine contamination that puts the Austrian diethylene glycol episode into the shade. Perhaps one should look further back for the warning signals to 1967, when nearly 300 Italians were charged in court, in one case, with manufacturing fake wine – allegedly from "water, sugar, ox blood, chemicals and the sludge from banana boats". The whole episode ended in farce. Not only was the case adjourned to allow the police further time to investigate but the "evidence", three-quarters of a million gallons of "wine", disappeared mysteriously while they were doing so. (One can only wonder at what you can do with all that liquid – it takes up rather a lot of space!) The trial was never resurrected.

The police were a little more alert in 1986, but you could argue that 22 dead Italian citizens was more than they could ignore. Two growers from the Piemonte region were charged first with manslaughter then murder, over a dozen producers were arrested and 30 firms were implicated. The scandal began in March that year when three people died after drinking wine laced with methyl alcohol. Police seized 5,000 bottles of cheap supermarket wine. Five more deaths followed, then 14,000 more bottles were seized and three ships carrying Italian wines were impounded by the French, who went on to destroy over a million litres of Italian wine. British holidaymakers were warned off drinking any cheap wine brought home after summer vacations, and most importing countries acted to prevent their citizens buying any doubtful wine.

Italy acted uncharacteristically quickly in attempting to stem the tide of their disappearing wine export trade, which was cut to 60% of the normal total. They admitted that their wine laws had been inadequate, and the Italian Government approved measures to combat lethal adulteration. Foreign buyers were compensated although the difficulty now involved in importing a small quantity of wine from Italy is being felt. For the organic wine producer with only a small quantity of his vintage to sell, export is now very unattractive. Every consignment of wine, whether a single bottle or a container load, must be accompanied by a health certificate costing the exporter approximately £50.

WINE SCANDALS

The Austrian diethylene glycol scandal was an attempt to profit by producing "better" wines commanding higher prices. In Italy the methyl alcohol scandal was an attempt to profit by producing an alcoholic drink so cheap that natural suspicions at the price would be overlooked in the search for cheap plonk. The Italian police believe the whole episode was a plan to defraud the EEC overproduction compensation system, but whichever nail you hammer in the coffin the fact cannot be escaped that innocent people died.

These scandals are not by any means the only ones in recent times, and before you relax in the absence of any French examples let us say there have been more than a few, notably the one uncovered by Nicholas Tomalin in *The Sunday Times* in the sixties where bulk wine was being labelled with any description the buyer cared to ask for. In our embarrassment as fooled wine drinkers it is only too easy to forget.

WHAT DOES ORGANIC WINE COST?

You will soon appreciate that at the expensive (say £5) end of the market an expensive bottle of organic wine is better value than its cheaper counterpart, not only in comparison to its chemical-laden alternative, but because of a number of unvariable costs. Each spring, the Chancellor announces the good or bad news about duty on alcoholic beverages. Wine-lovers can be more optimistic nowadays as we try to come more in line with cheaper prices on the Continent. But how much duty do you pay? As of summer 1987 excise duty on a 70cl bottle is 68·6 pence, 73·5 pence on a 75cl bottle, 98 pence on a half-litre and £1·21 for 75cl of sparkling wine, including champagne. You can cope with that? Fine, but what else do you fork out for?

British Value Added Tax is 15% today, and the unlucky wine merchant has to pay it the minute the wine clears customs, not after he's sold it to you and has a few free nights to do his VAT returns. You have to pay for customs clearance: everything we import needs a tariff code entered on to importation documents, and the clearance agent wants his fee. Insurance must be covered while the wine is in transit (as well as in the seller's cellars) and bank charges will be paid when you have your pounds sterling sent abroad, currency converted, to the producer's bank account.

The largest lump, however, after duty, is the transport

WHAT DOES ORGANIC WINE COST?

charge. It is very expensive to drive cases of wine all through the French road system, and one can count on anything from 25p upwards per bottle. (It is in fact cheaper to ship a bottle of sake from Japan to the UK than to haul a bottle of claret overland.)

In short: 73·5p (duty), 30p (haulage), 5p (customs clearance, bank + insurance) = £1·08·5. If the wine costs £1, that's £2·08·5, then the merchant's mark-up – it may be notoriously low but he must make a profit, say 16·6% – and your one bottle costs £2·50, plus 15% VAT = £2·87. That's before the merchant sells it to a retailer and he in turn has to make a margin, another 16·6%. This bottle now costs £3·45.

The better-known wines also carry a hefty advertising charge – Piat d'Or are said to spend up to £1 a bottle; subtract that and the aforementioned charges from the retail price and that leaves . . . well, does it leave anything for the wine?

Here's hoping you can carry it home and don't need a bank loan to keep it in your cellar for the next decade, but if you choose to enjoy it in a restaurant – expect to pay at least £5-£6 before service charge for this same bottle.

FRANCE

France sets the standards by which all other wines are judged. Claret, red and white Burgundy, the wines of Alsace, the Rhône and the Loire, Champagne all attain a degree of depth and sophistication only occasionally found in the wines of the rest of the world. This is not to put down German wines from the Rhine, Riojas from Spain, Barolos from Italy and some stunners from California and Australia; but for overall diversity and finesse France cannot be beaten. The first wine vines were introduced around Marseilles by the Greeks or perhaps earlier by the Carthaginians from North Africa. Certainly, by the time the Romans had colonised it vines were being established along the Rhône up to Burgundy and westwards along the Garonne towards Bordeaux. The Romans developed vines more suited to the comparatively cooler summers and colder winters than they were used to in Italy or Spain, and although the vintages varied from year to year they much preferred the higher quality. By the fourth century vineyards had spread as far north as Paris, the Moselle and Normandy.

Through the unfortunately named Dark Ages new wine strains were developed, forests were cleared, land was drained and new pruning techniques turned the once sprawling vine into the more bush-like shape we now know.

Even although the wooden cask had been known for centuries it was only in the relatively damper climate of France, where they did not so frequently dry out and crack, that they were used for storing wine. The wine could be kept for a longer period without wasting, it developed a finer flavour and of course it could be transported more easily.

FRANCE

By the 16th century viticulture was a recognised skill and experimentation into new strains of grapes and methods was positively encouraged. By the 18th century French wines were the world leaders exporting to North America, Scandinavia and the Orient. Britain, regardless of wars with France, managed one way or another to maintain supplies of its favourite (unfortified) wines.

Napoleonic reforms had in many respects improved the French wine world and André Simon writes in his *The noble grapes and the great wines of France*, "There was in all probability, more and finer wines made in France from 1830 to 1880 than had ever been made before from all the vineyards in the world. Wines were so good and there were so much of them in that blessed half century that they could be, and often had to be, kept; they were thus given a chance to show how great they could be."

They say syphilis may have spread from the New World but the vine equivalent certainly did. *Phylloxera vastatrix* (the vine louse) was first noticed in Provence in the 1860s and by 1890 had spread as far north as Champagne. In America the local vine, *Vitis labrusca*, lives in relative harmony with the creature which lives mostly on its leaves. In France, however, *Vitis vinifera* did not have the same root resistance; the louse attacked these roots which slowly killed the whole plant. The effect was disastrous. People were forced to sell their vineyards, if they could, the workers left the land and, moreover, there was little wine to drink or sell.

During this period there were a number of wine scandals. Foreign wine was regularly labelled as, or mixed in with, recognised French wines and many poor thin wines were chemically improved.

The antidote to *phylloxera* was to graft the French vines on to American rootstocks and replant, but this was a very expensive process and nearly half the vineyards were never replanted. One of the few benefits of this whole episode was that plantings and layout could be rethought and rationalised. As the vineyards were replanted the growers were justifiably upset at the sale of phony wines under existing names, especially if they had spent a lot of time and money recreating the original. After

THE ORGANIC WINE GUIDE

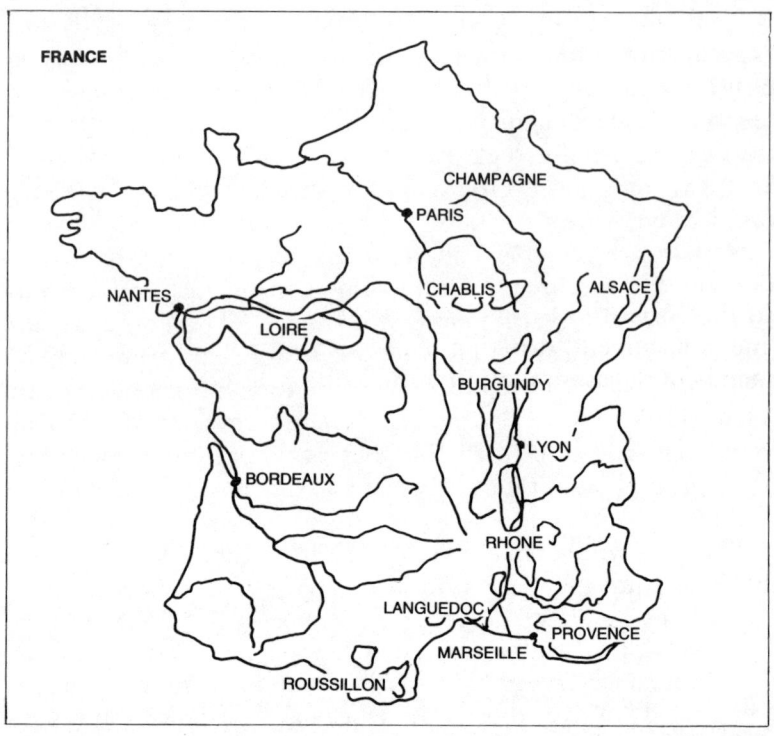

a long struggle the Institut National des Appellations d'Origine des Vins et Eaux-de-Vie was set up in 1932, commonly referred to as the INAO.

Essentially there are now four categories of French wine:

Appellation Controlé or Appellation d'Origine Controlé (AC or AOC)

This controls grape varieties used, vinification methods, alcohol levels, and permitted yield per hectare; as we shall see, these controls and standards vary from region to region. Originally designed to provide a guarantee of authenticity, an attempt is now being made to control quality by tasting.

Vin Délimité de Qualité Supérieure (VDQS)

The second division, used for areas with a special identity. Again controls are imposed on grapes used etc. but generally a greater yield her hectare is allowed plus greater flexibility in alcoholic strength.

Vins de Pays
It translates as country wine but perhaps vin ordinaire from a specific region gives a better idea. Supposedly inferior to VDQS, they can be very good and again they are controlled as to grapes, strength and by tasting.

Vin de Consommation Courante
Wine for current drinking and not controlled. The price depends on local reputation and alcoholic strength.

As far as the EEC is concerned wine is either a Vin de Qualité Produit dans une Région Déterminée (VQPRD) or a vin de table.

The organic standards which may be found on French wine are Nature et Progrès, Terre et Vie, Lemaire Boucher (Terre-Océan being the conversion symbol) and Demeter for biodynamic production, that is grapes that have been grown and harvested in harmony with the cycles of astral bodies and the moon. People using the biodynamic method may just say "biodynamique" (Bio Dynamique, Bio-dynamic, Biodynamie) or append it to one of the above.

ALSACE

Viticulture was established in Alsace by the Romans and after the setback of a Germanic invasion in the fifth century the development of the area was continued by the Church. It is said to have reached a peak in the late 16th century and there are certainly some magnificent houses from this period. The Thirty Years War (1618-1648) caused a lot of damage to the region and when they got round to replanting they tended to use low-quality varieties. A Royal Edict of 1731 and the aftermath of the French Revolution did not succeed in encouraging a growth in quality although production did increase.

A number of factors influenced the generally bad reputation

of wine from Alsace, namely the glut of poor quality wine, *phylloxera*, a swing to beer-drinking and the willingness of Germany to absorb large quantities for blending and cheap fizz.

Since World War II the growers, co-operatives and producer/shippers have made an enormous effort to acquire a reputation for quality, and in this they have very largely succeeded. The most obvious characteristic of an Alsace wine is its flowery bouquet and secondly its crispness, reliability and reasonable price. There is a similarity to German wines but they are fully fermented out, retaining their fragrance but tasting much drier. The minimum permitted alcohol level is 8·5% but sugar can be added before fermentation (chaptalisation); probably because the French are accustomed to white wine having a strength of 11% this can be up to 12·5%.

In Alsace the Appellation Contrôlée categories are done by grape variety, predominantly Riesling, Gewurztraminer, Sylvaner, Tokay d'Alsace (Pinot Gris), Pinot Noir, Pinot (Pinot Blanc sometimes known as Klevner and Auxerrois Blanc) and Muscat. The exception to this rule is called Edelzwicker, a blend of several grapes including the local Chasselas; popular in Alsace, it can vary in quality in other countries.

Two special categories were authorised in 1984, Vendanges Tardives and Sélection des Grains Nobles. They are both made from late-picked, very ripe grapes sometimes with noble rot, with the Sélection des Grains Nobles requiring a higher alcohol level. Needless to say they are very expensive because of the labour intensity required and their rarity.

In good years there are other wines that benefit from ageing even although the received wisdom is that Alsace wines should be drunk young; the two best examples would be the Rieslings and the Gewurztraminers.

Growers seldom do their own pressing and vinification and usually send their product to a co-operative, large estate or one of the producer/shippers, with the result that there are fewer opportunities for the organic grower than in, say, the Midi. It must be admitted that firms like Dopff et Irion are very

FRANCE – ALSACE

light-handed with the sulphur dioxide and have invested large sums in creating sterile areas using inert gas. Many Alsacean wine makers are very strongly principled.

In that the wines of Alsace are labelled by grape variety we have decided to list the makers alphabetically rather than each individual wine.

GAEC Pierre Frick et Fils
Nature et Progrès/Bio-dynamic. 50,000 bottles overall p.a. 66Hl/hectare.
5 Rue de Baer, 68250 Pfaffenheim, Haut-Rhin, ALSACE. tel 89 49 62 99

The Fricks have been making wine for five generations and have been using organic methods since 1970. In 1981 they began using the biodynamic cultivation method and since 1986 have been entitled to use the title 'Demeter'. Their reasons for using these methods are particularly straightforward: they wish to respect the environment, not work with anything toxic and produce a wine of better quality. All their wines get a light oak maturation and are not treated by chemical or physical means, so they are still alive in the bottle and may therefore throw a slight sediment or develop a slight petillance. The wines they produce are Sylvaner, Edelzwicker, Chasselas, Klevner, Pinot Blanc, Riesling, Muscat, Tokay d'Alsace/Pinot Gris, Pinot Noir and Gewurztraminer.

Eugène Meyer
Demeter (Syndicat d'Agriculture Bio-Dynamique)
Berholtz, Haut-Rhin, ALSACE.

Muscat '85 A pronounced rich nose led on to a slightly dry mouthful that developed into something richer on the aftertaste. This was generally liked.

Riesling '85 Disappointing on the nose, it was sharp and distinctly dry and two tasters expressed a desire for more fruit.

Tokay '86 This was the favourite out of the Meyer tasting. Warm toast and citrus were followed by full fruit and almonds;

THE ORGANIC WINE GUIDE

a hint of pepper and splendidly dry, this also had a satisfying finish.

ANDRÉ STENTZ
Nature et Progrès. 10-15,000 bottles p.a. 40-100 Hl/hectare. 2 Rue de la Batteuse, 68920 Wettolsheim, Haut-Rhin, ALSACE. tel 89 80 64 91

Andrè Stentz has been encouraged in his personal desire to improve the environment by his friends and clients; the improvement of their health and the quality of the wine follow. He produces the following wines: Edelzwicker, Sylvaner, Pinot Blanc, Riesling, Tokay d'Alsace, Muscat, Gewurztraminer, Pinot Noir, Crêmant d'Alsace and we append the following tasting notes:

Edelzwicker '86 This had a curious nose, reminded some of sake and licorice, and although one person thought it well made "given the grapes" (basically Chasselas) it was generally liked.

FRANCE – ALSACE

Gewurztraminer-Steingrubler '83 Immediately recognisable, this delighted the nose and was praised for not being overstated but definitely satisfying; overall a mouth-filling wine, pungent and delicious.

Riesling '86 With a good oily nose and good fruit, this was considered solid and rustic but with such racy acidity it is not for people with ulcers.

Tokay d'Alsace '83 A short nose led on to a wine described variously as unbalanced, heavy, awkward and ungainly.

RICHARD WURTZ-SIGRIST
Nature et Progrès
8 Rue de Buhl, 68630 Mittelwihr Benwhir, ALSACE. tel 89 47 90 67

BORDEAUX

Bordeaux is arguably the most important wine region in the world. Apart from the wine itself the main reasons for this are its history, climate and soil. It produces lots of light reds and whites but is most famous for the slow-maturing reds and luscious sweet whites.

Before vines were planted by the Romans Bordeaux imported wine from Italy and served as a distribution centre for the area and with the marriage of Eleanor of Aquitaine and Henry Plantagenet in 1152 the trade with Britain and the rest of Northern Europe was put on a firmer footing. Today Bordeaux accounts for 33% of all appellation contrôlée exports from France.

Originally the red wines were called "vins clairets" to distinguish them from the heavier Iberian wines and now, at least in English-speaking countries, it is referred to as claret. The wines that we now know began to be developed during the 18th century as British shippers bought the young wines and began ageing them in oak barrels and after a while bottling them for sale. The development of the cork, the sterilising effects of sulphur dioxide and the preserving qualities of the tannin from the grapes and the barrels all contributed to the process. The consumer too helped by recognising certain wines, "And here drank a sort of French wine called Ho Bryan, that hath a good and most particular taste that I have never met with" – Pepys in the spring of 1663.

The weather goes a long way in explaining the enormous interest taken in the different vintages. Having a maritime climate the weather can be very cold in April, which can freeze and damage the emerging buds. In June there can be cold, wet weather which can inhibit proper pollination, a misfortune known as "coulure". Yet the warm sunny autumns can bring the fruit to full ripeness, saving a potentially bad year or adding the finishing touch to a glorious year.

There is a lot of research and debate going on about the contribution that the soil makes to the wine, but I think it is generally accepted that whether it is gravel or limestone good drainage is important to encourage the roots to go deeper and thus come into contact with a greater number of trace elements (organic soil helps provide these trace elements). In Bordeaux the red wines are made mainly from Cabernet Sauvignon, Cabernet Franc and Merlot with dashes of Petit Verdot and Malbec. Surprisingly Cabernet Sauvignon was only introduced at the end of the 18th century and although it is the key element in the quality reds and resistant to rot (important in a damp climate) it still only accounts for 18% of plantings on the available land. Sauvignon is the principal white grape along with Semillon. Muscadelle is not so popular and there is a lot of recent planting with Ugni Blanc (Trebbiano) which gives a good yield but is essentially dull. Semillon is the most important grape used for the sweet wines of Sauterne and Barsac. For once rot is encouraged, and in this instance the botrytis known as "pourriture noble" which affects the grape by piercing the skin with tiny threads of fungus which allow the juices to slowly evaporate, thus concentrating the sugar and flavour. This produces a dessert wine of luscious complexity.

Several factors can make it difficult to find your way round the wines of the region, for example many people wonder how there are so many wines called Château This or Château That. Are all the wine-makers that rich? In practice "château" refers to an estate or "marque", not necessarily a defined piece of land or a grand house. Field definition is not considered to be of supreme importance in Bordeaux because the wine-maker has so many decisions to make each and every year, not to mention the importance of reputation.

People also get confused with the different ways of classifying wines within the region. In 1855 the wines of the Médoc (with the exception of Château Haut-Brion from Graves) were divided into five groups – Premier Crus, Deuxièmes Crus and so on. This was based on the price each wine had received over a period of years and is still used today although it is a great source of debate. The unclassed wines of the Médoc can be Cru Bourgeois, Cru Grand Bourgeois and Cru Grand Bourgeois Exceptionnel.

Other areas have their own classifications and methods, for example Saint Émilion where the wines are classified regularly into Premiers Grands Crus Classés A, Premiers Grand Crus Classés B, Grands Crus Classés and Grand Cru. To further confuse there are no vins de pays or VDQS wines, only AOC Bordeaux, AOC Bordeaux Supérieurs, and they can add the name of the district, e.g. Bordeaux Côtes de Costillon. We constantly refer to more specialist books on the subject and we suggest you do too if this is an area that interests you.

LA BEYLIE. BORDEAUX AC. r.w
Terre et Vie
Jean-Paul Richard, La Beylie, 33220 Les Lèves, GIRONDE. tel 57 46 31 28

The white wine is called Ste. Foy.

BOURASSON, VIN DE TABLE. r
Nature et Progrès
Jean-Luc Devert, St. Quentin de Caplong, 33220 Ste. Foy La Grande, GIRONDE. tel 57 46 36 13

CHÂTEAU BALLUE MONDON, BORDEAUX AC. r.w
Lemaire-Boucher. 48,000 bottles p.a.
Guy Ballue, 33890 Gensac, GIRONDE. tel 57 40 42 25

These wines are made high up on the slopes of the Gironde.

'83 Nice full fruity flavour and lots of tannin. Mouth-filling now but should keep.

'82 The white we tasted split the company. We all liked the sherbety nose but the women found it "thin on the palate" with "a bitter aftertaste" whereas the men found it "nicely controlled alcohol"; "gooseberry and grapefruit" and "a classic Sauvignon".

CHÂTEAU BARRAIL DES GRAVES. SAINT ÉMILION AC. r
Nature et Progrès. 25,000 bottles p.a.
GAEC Descrambes, Saint Sulpice de Faleyrens, 33330 Saint Émilion. tel 57 74 94 77

FRANCE – BORDEAUX

This vineyard has been in the family for three generations and the decision to go organic was taken by Gérard Descrambes' father in 1950. Gérard, a serious wine-maker, is not without a sense of humour – witness the occasional designer label commissioned from a few famous cartoonists. The grapes planted are Cabernet Sauvignon 20%, Merlot 60%, Cabernet Franc 15% and Malbec 5%. The wine is fermented with the grapes' own yeast at a strictly controlled temperature of between 28 and 31 degrees, and after fermentation it is treated only by physical methods, i.e. lowering the temperature and filtering both before and after a maturing period of six to eight months in oak casks.

'82 "Real claret" colour beginning to soften at the edges and a touch of anaesthetic strength on the nose. Soft and plummy on the palate with overtones of strawberry. Drinkable now but

perhaps deceptively so. A tannin fur on the teeth indicates keeping. It has a lovely long aftertaste.

THE ORGANIC WINE GUIDE

Château Bosseut. AC Bordeaux Supérieur. r
Exploitations Dubost, St. Denis-de-Pile, 33500; Libourne, GIRONDE. tel 57 51 76 57

'82 Generally well liked and most tasters used words like "balanced", "smooth" and "drinkable" although somebody found the taste "alarming", veering between sourness and fruit.

Château Busqueyron. Bordeaux Supérieur AC. r.w
Lemaire-Boucher
René Maugey, 33750 Saint Germain-du-Puch, GIRONDE. tel 56 24 55 34

With a history dating back to the 14th century this estate produces not only a red but also a very aromatic dry white, unusual for an Entre-deux-Mers.

Château Chavrignac. AC. r
Nature et Progrès. 40,000 bottles p.a.
GAEC Paul Bouron et fils, Fosses et Baleyssac, 33190 La Réole, GIRONDE. tel 56 61 70 50

'83 This had a complex, aromatic nose and a full, well-balanced flavour and showed some style.

Château Chouteau. AC Saint Émilion. Grand Cru. r
Lemaire-Boucher

Michel Rogerie

Château de Prade. Bordeaux Supérieur Côtes de Castillon AC. r
Lemaire-Boucher
Isnel Fournier, Belves-de-Castillon, 33350 Castillon-La-Bataille, GIRONDE. tel 56 40 19 73

Isnel Fournier has been fully organic since 1970 and apart from the red also makes a rosé.

'83 Lovely mature colour with orange at the edge. Concentrated ripe saucy nose, one enthusiast found "woodland flowers and sandalwood". Wild superb texture although there were one or two reservations about a touch of metal. Some Castillons age very quickly and this was no exception.

CHÂTEAU DES HAUTES COMBE. BORDEAUX AC. r
GAEC Delfarge-Garcia

'85 Bright red, purply pink at the edge, showing its youth with legs on the glass which is not surprising given the 12.6%

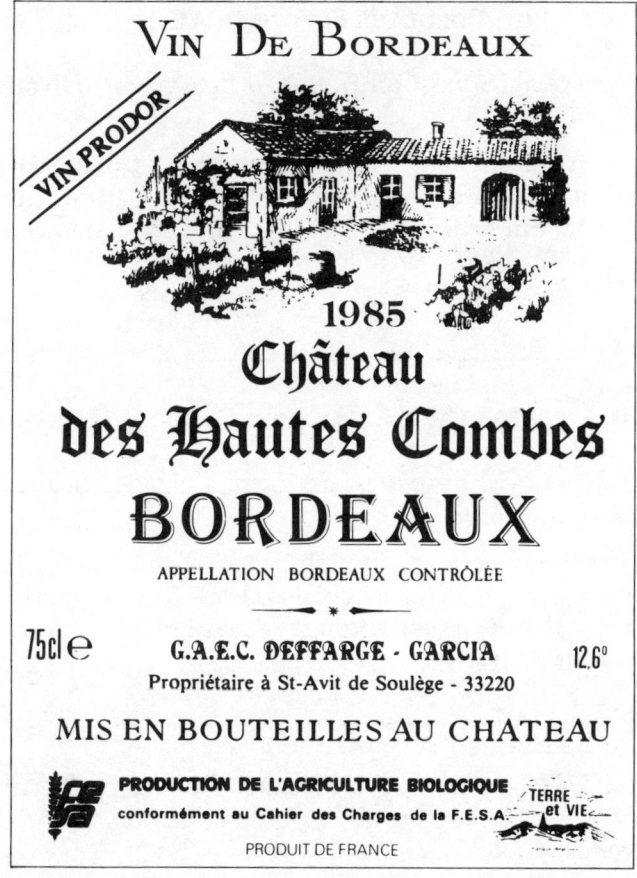

alcohol. Not much tannin and a pronounced cherry taste gives an almost Gamay feel. Best to drink young as a nouveau-type wine.

THE ORGANIC WINE GUIDE

Château du Moulin de Peyronin. Bordeaux AC. r

'85 Youthful purply colour, the tasters used dried fig, juniper berries, nutmeg and blackcurrant to describe the nose. Excellent fruit and tannin suggest that this well-constructed wine will improve.

Château du Puy. Bordeaux Supérieur AC. r
Terre-Océan
Robert Amoreau, Saint-Cibart, 33570 Lussac, GIRONDE. tel 57 40 61 06

'81 Light mature colour shot with yellow and orange with a spicy, woody, slightly sharp nose. Plenty of mature fruit but not much tannin or finish. There was an impression that the wine was maturing too early but we will certainly be checking out the other vintages.

Château Jacques Blanc. St Émilion Grand CRU AC. r
Nature et Progrès
Pierre Chouet, St. Étiennes de Lisse, 33330 St. Émilion, GIRONDE. tel 57 40 18 01

'82 Very pale amber colour, much lighter than expected for an '82. A touch of resin on the lovely nose leads on to a mouthful of good fruit with oak coming through. A wine of inherent quality but just a bit edgy.

Château La Mirandole, AC Premières Côtes de Blaye. r
Paul Berjon et Mme, Braud-et-Saint-Louis, 33820 St-Ciers-sur-Gironde, GIRONDE

'79 Beginning to show age at the edges, this should be drunk now. With a lovely sedate blackcurrant nose, it has obvious quality although light in style.

FRANCE – BORDEAUX

CHÂTEAU LES JÉSUITES. BORDEAUX AC. r
Lemaire-Boucher. 20,000 bottles p.a. 50 Hl/hectare
Guy Lucmaret, Saint-Maixant, 33490 Saint-Macaire, GIRONDE. tel 56 63 17 97

Guy Lucmaret has been making his wines since 1968 and offers his clients a chemical-free wine because of his "amour de la Nature".

'84 Has a concentrated purply colour with a bummy nose developing into something more pleasantly aromatic. Hard, astringent, tannic but good fruit suggests this wine should develop well.

'83 No softness in the colour yet and a farmyard, woody smell that becomes very attractive. Still tannic but plenty fruit ranging from citrus to soft. Drinking well now but will keep.

'82 Lighter colour than the above wines with cherry at the edges. A flattish nose, hints of leather and round fruit in the mouth. Drink now. Everybody liked this above-average petit château.

CHÂTEAU MÉRIC. GRAVES AC. r. GRAVES SUPÉRIEURE AC w
Nature et Progrès. 50-60,000 bottles p.a. 45 Hl/hectare
P. Barron, 33650 La Brède, GIRONDE. tel 56 20 20 53

Monsieur Barron is proud of the fact that his family have been making wine for centuries and advises us to "drink little but drink well, drink natural wine in order to drink for a long time". He makes the white wine from 50% Semillon, 40% Sauvignon and 10% Muscadelle. The reds comprise 50% Merlot, 26% Cabernet Franc, 15% Cabernet Sauvignon and 9% Malbec.

'85 r This has an enticing raspberry and blackcurrant bouquet and a youthful complex ripe fruitiness with not too much tannin. It has a long aftertaste with cloves predominating.

'86 w Strongly perfumed, reminding one taster of clover honey, this wine proved to be rather insipid, probably a result of so much Semillon. Another taster thought it a typical Graves Supérieure and a good example of what it was.

THE ORGANIC WINE GUIDE

CHÂTEAU MOULIN DE ROMAGE. BORDEAUX AC. r.w.sw.w
Terre-Océan
Alain Piroux, Les Lèves et Thoumeyragues, 33220 Ste Foy La Grande, GIRONDE. tel 57 46 45 99

'86 w One heroic taster noted lemon blossom and marmalade. However, the general consensus was that it did not have much taste and what there was faded in the mouth.

'86 sw w Nice spicy open nose leading on to a medium-sweet wine with soft, slightly smoky fruit and an attractive slaty finish. It reminded us of some Sauternes and Vouvrays.

FRANCE – BORDEAUX

'86 r Shocking crimson/purple colour and a fruity nose without any definition. In the mouth it was jammy and supple and typical of the large '86 vintage. A good petit château wine for drinking now.

'85 r Bright pinky purple in appearance, this is a wine of good tannin and acidity with subdued but suave fruitiness which needs time.

CHÂTEAU PETIT ROC. BORDEAUX AC. r.w
Groupement des Agriculteurs Biologistes du Sud-Ouest
Jean-Paul Richard, Les Lèves, 33220 Ste-Foy-La-Grande, GIRONDE. tel 57 41 20 28

'85 r This had a very dark, black/purple colour and a nose that evoked leather, animals, mildew, seaweed, burnt rubber and cherries. It was mouth-puckeringly tannic with lots of fruit, was almost Rhône-like and "screams of youth". One taster reckoned there was probably an element of Petit Verdot in it to discourage too early consumption.

'85 w Washed-out brass and straw were used to describe this wine's appearance and toasted Sauvignon to describe the nose. There was lovely fresh acidity, overtones of apples and lemons, and it would make good summer drinking, if not too chilled.

FRANCE – BORDEAUX

Château Renaissance. Bordeaux AC. r
Nature et Progrès. 30,000 bottles p.a.
GAEC Descrambes, Saint-Sulpice-de-Faleyrens, 33330 Saint Émilion, GIRONDE. tel 57 74 94 77

This wine is from the same stable as Château Barrail des Graves.

'85 Of medium colour, this has a light nose with a hint of Malbec smokiness. It is supple and balanced with a lot of warmth and charm. Somebody noted roast venison and another a long berry finish.

Château Saint-Hilaire. Graves AC. r.w
Terre et Océan. 25,000 bottles p.a. 40-45 Hl/hectare
Gabriel Guérin, Castres, 33640 Portets, GIRONDE. tel 56 67 12 12

Gabriel Guérin has been making wine using the Lemaire-Boucher method since 1964 because he considers it to produce a wine of better quality. For the reds he uses Merlot, Malbec and Cabernet Sauvignon and for the whites a blend of Semillon and Sauvignon. The reds are matured in oak casks for 18 months.

Chic de Balzurie. Méthode Champenoise. w
Lemaire-Boucher
Guy Ballue, 33890 Gensac, GIRONDE. tel 57 40 42 25

A white sparkler from the makers of Château Ballue Mondon.

Chic de Balzurie. Méthode Champenoise. w
Lemaire-Boucher
Guy Ballue, 33890 Gensac, GIRONDE. tel 57 40 42 25

NV w Our only quibble with this attractive wine was that although it had an appealing yeasty nose it was maybe lacking in fruit or vinous aromas.

THE ORGANIC WINE GUIDE

CLOS DE LA PÉRICHÈRE. GRAVES AC. r.w
Terre et Océan. 15,000 bottles p.a. 40-45 Hl/hectare
Gabriel Guerin, Castres, 33640 Portets, GIRONDE. tel 56 67 12 12

Made by the makers of Château Saint-Hilaire, both the red and white are marginally cheaper.

CLOS GRAND PLANTIER. BORDEAUX SUPÉRIEUR AC. r.w
Terre et Vie
Magniéval Frères, Vérac, 33240 St-André-de-Cubzac, GIRONDE. tel 57 84 42 96

CLOS LA MAURASSE. AC GRAVES r.w
Terre-Océan. 24,000 bottles p.a.
R. Sessacq, Clos La Maurasse, 33210 Langon, GIRONDE. tel 56 63 20 24

'85 w Slightly austere on the nose, this was a sound, typical white Graves with gravelly, metallic undertones. Somebody said if you like this style of wine you will like this one.

'83 r This had a lovely "tannic red" colour, a "good burnt blackcurrant nose" and an earthy, almost tobacco flavour that was well liked by all.

CLOS LAURIOLE. BORDEAUX LUPÉRIEUR AC. r.w
Nature et Progrès. 46,500 bottles p.a. 50 Hl/hectare
Jean-François Mauros, Île Saint Georges, 33640 Portets, GIRONDE. tel 56 67 15 45

Jean-François Mauros has been making organic wine for 15 years as a response to the publicity given to the damaging effects of pesticides and because of his philosophy that quality should replace quantity.

'85 r This wine had a youthful colour but not a lot of depth. It was meaty, well balanced and a potentially good wine. Unfortunately the sample we tasted was corked. Several people mentioned nuts both at the beginning and the end.

FRANCE – BORDEAUX

CLOS LE MAS. BORDEAUX SUPÉRIEUR AC. r.w
Lemaire-Boucher. 17,000 bottles p.a.
Michel Rogerie, Petit Palais, 33570 Lussac, GIRONDE. tel 57 74 65 85

'82 r A beautiful rich red turning amber at the edges with a typical blackcurrant nose, this wine was liked by everyone for its well-balanced depth, full fruit and excellent finish.

'83 r A deep bouquet was not hinted at by the just maturing medium-weight colour, lots of fruit, oak and a touch of rottenness.

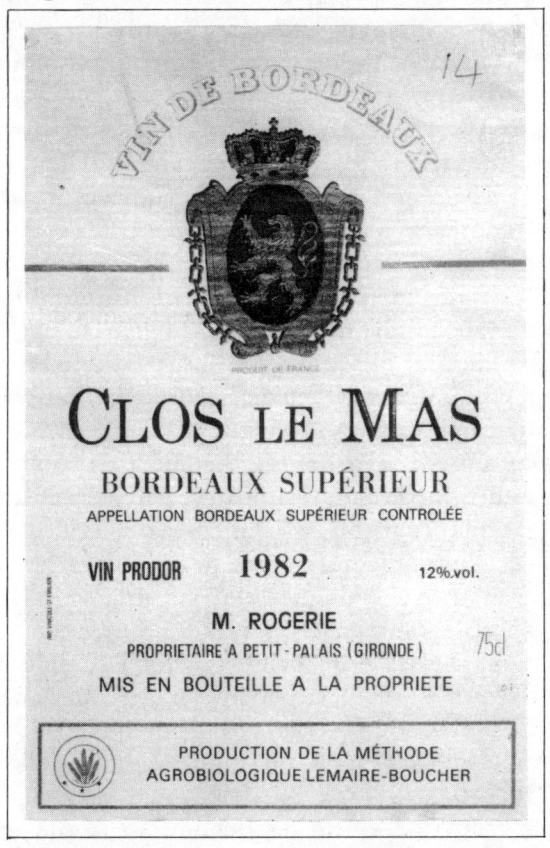

Lovely fruit/oak balance and a dry tannic aftertaste of some length produced the comments "satisfying mouthful" and "lipsmacking".

BURGUNDY

From the middle of the first millennium AD to the middle of the second millennium AD Burgundy was a separate kingdom or duchy often at war with the rest of France. It stretched as far north as the Low Countries and from the Loire in the west to the Jura in the east. Nowadays it can only be defined as a specific region in terms of wine and perhaps food; known as the belly of France, it has a very large number of highly rated restaurants and is especially famous for Charolais beef, Bresse chickens and snails. Geographically it now stretches from Chablis in the Yonne in the north to Lyons in the south.

The vineyards are mostly smallholdings owned by peasant proprietors and this situation came about when the large Church estates were split up after the Revolution and then were further fragmented as a result of the French law of inheritance which states that all property be divided equally among the offspring. This means that the bulk of Burgundy wines is bought by a négociant by the barrel and sold as the product of a given village. district or vineyard. The most cited example of this is Clos de Vougeot which has more than 50 proprietors owning patches of varying quality.

Chablis is the wine made in the most northern part of Burgundy and is world famous for dry, pale, crisp, flinty-taste wines that do not become overly fat and opulent because of the climate. Travelling south, we come to the Côte d'Or, so called either because it is a golden slope or because it faces east (Orient), which comprises the Côte de Nuit, about 12 miles long, and then the Côte de Beaune, which is about twice as large. The world's most expensive wine, Romanée-Conti, comes from the Côte de Nuit as well as such truly classic wines as Échezaux, La Tache and the more regularly encountered Nuits St Georges.

The reds from the Côtes de Beaune are softer and more delicate, such as Le Corton, Savigny-Les-Beaunes and Beaune itself. This is also where the fabulous white burgundies come from – Puligny-Montrachet and Meursault being two giants.

FRANCE – BURGUNDY

Here the communes or villages often link their names to the most illustrious vineyard, thus you get Chassagne-Montrachet which may sound grander to an English consumer but is, in fact, inferior. The Challonais follows on, boasting of such wines as Mercurey, Montagny, Rully and Givry. All wines in Burgundy are expensive but these are a little less so. The Maconnais, further down, is most famous for its white Pouilly-Fuisse but others such as Saint-Véran and Macon Vire are more reasonable alternatives.

Then, to the north of Lyons we have Beaujolais; suffering, perhaps, from overexposure due to the annual brouhaha surrounding Beaujolais Nouveau and its constantly mentioned quaffability. It is a less serious wine than most Burgundy but it is made from a different grape (the Gamay), often has a silky sophistication and some do, in fact, age remarkably well, e.g. Moulin à Vent.

Modern methods of wine-making are being introduced all the time. However, traditional methods and beliefs are still strongly held. Traditionally the wines are left in the vats, on the lees to clear themselves, unless the vats are needed for the new harvest. It is believed that the wine gets troubled three times a year, i.e. when the vine buds, when it flowers and when the grapes ripen. The wine is considered to throw a sediment at these times and it is thought best if this happens in the vat. It is also thought that the south wind, the "Vent du Midi", troubles the wine, so bottling is only done when the wind is in the north and the moon is on the wane.

Burgundy is different from the rest of France in that the majority of the production is made from only two grapes, Chardonnay for the major whites and Pinot Noir for the whites. Beaujolais uses the Gamay for its distinctive reds and the Aligote is used for the lighter whites throughout the region but it is the first two grapes that give the region the reputation that is only equalled by Bordeaux. Like claret the Pinot Noir is matured in oak but matures more quickly and does not have the same amount of tannin; but like claret it does require some bottle age to soften it up and bring it together.

The grapes are crushed in a mill and placed in an open-topped cuve or vat, and whether they are fermented with the stalks and for how long depends on the sort of wine, longevity and style that is required. In centuries past, if the must was too cool to start a good fermentation, the farmhands stripped off and jumped into the vat to add the heat of their bodies (and what else?) to speed the process. Heated coils now take the place of the more organic method.

Chaptalisation is standard practice in Burgundy where it is generally considered to produce a better fermentation and a better wine, but no more than enough to produce 2% alcohol by volume. The 1981 regulations state that ordinary Burgundy must have at least 10% alcohol so this could be legally raised to 12%. This is not always necessary with white wines as they can reach 13% naturally.

Because Chablis is cooler than the Côte d'Or large vats are used to ferment the Chardonnay; but because a slow fermentation is preferred to maintain maximum freshness in the Côte d'Or they use small barrels to limit a build-up of temperature. They also sometimes use fresh oak barrels in order to add pungency right at the beginning of the process. When the fermentation is finished the wine is left in the barrels until clear, racked into clean barrels and then bottled. Hugh Johnson in his admirable *Wine Companion* comments on white Burgundy: "An ideally balanced vintage keeps a tension between the increasingly rich flavours of maturity and a central steeliness, year after year".

In Burgundy, the Côte d'Or and Chablis have an appellation system with about 30 Grands Crus, e.g. Les Clos, Grenouilles, Le Corton and Le Montrachet; then there are the Premiers Crus where the vineyard can be printed on the label the same size as the commune. These are followed by an Appellation Contrôlée Communale which can use the commune/village name or the vineyard or both, but the vineyard name must be half the size on the label; and then the Appellations Régionales, e.g. Bourgogne and Bourgogne Aligote.

BEAUJOLAIS AC. r
Nature et Progrès. 5,000 bottles p.a. 55 Hl/hectare
Gérard Belaid, La Roche du Puy, 69910 Villie-Morgon, RHONE. tel 74 69 13 36

Gérard and his sister are the son and daughter wine-growers and are in the process of creating their own business. They are using Nature et Progrès to obtain a better product and to create a more agreeable and enriching work-style.

NV This had an obvious Gamay nose but in the mouth there was a tinny sweetness and an insubstantial body.

BEAUJOLAIS AC. r
Biodynamie. 20-25,000 bottles p.a. 50-55 Hl/hectare
René Bosse Platière, Les Carrières, Lucenay, 69480 Anse, RHONE. tel 74 67 00 99

René Bosse Platière started making wine in 1945 on land that has belonged to his family since 1758. Since 1958 he had been looking for ways to produce wine that was different from those recommended in the "official literature" and their "so-called progress", and in 1968 he got poisoned while killing weeds. He rigorously goes by Maria Thun's planetary calendar and no longer uses any fertiliser in his vineyard whether organic or mineral. Any vegetation springing up between June and November is added to the prunings from the vines and they form an "autofertilisation" which allows him to reach the production authorised by the Appellation authorities. He stopped using Bordeaux mixture ten years ago.

BEAUJOLAIS. AC. r
Jean-Paul Lagoutte, St. Julien/Bibost, 69690 Bessenay, RHONE

BEAUJOLAIS RÉGNIE AC. BEAUJOLAIS VILLAGES. r
Nature et Progrès. 1,500 bottles p.a. 40-60 Hl/hectare
André Rampon, Vernus, Régnie-Durette, 69430 Beaujeu, RHONE. tel 74 04 34 58

From 1988 this will be known as Cru Régnie and André Rampon is going to increase his annual production. He has been making wine since 1970 and uses organic methods for "flavour and out of conviction".

BEAUNE-PREMIER CRU. AC. r
Biodynamie/Nature et Progrès. 5,000 bottles p.a. 45 Hl/hectare
Pierrette et Jean-Claude Rateau, Chemin des Mariages, 21200 Beaune, COTE D'OR. tel 80 22 52 54

Pierrette and Jean-Claude Rateau are looking for viable long-term techniques to produce quality products, a balanced plant physiology, to stop the downgrading of the environment, to avoid the appearance of new parasites created by resistance to chemical cultivation techniques, and to these ends they started organic cultivation on 1st January 1979. They make several other wines which are listed separately in this chapter. They use Pinot Noir for the red and Chardonnay for the white.

BEAUNE-CLOS DES MARIAGES AC. r
Biodynamie/Nature et Progrès. 5,000 bottles p.a. 45 Hl/hectare
Pierrette et Jean-Claude Rateau, Chemin des Mariages, 21200 Beaune, COTE D'OR. tel 80 22 52 54

BOURGOGNE AC. r
Lemaire-Boucher. 45,000 bottles p.a. 50-60 Hl/hectare
André Chaumont, St Jean de Vaux, 71640 Givry, SAONE ET LOIRE. tel 85 45 13 77

Although he had a classical training from studying at the Beaune school of viticulture he soon realised that chemicals helped to increase production to the detriment of quality, thereby accentuating parasitism, and this led to an increase in his use of phyto-sanitary products rather than synthetic chemicals. Although he started using the Lemaire-Boucher method in 1965 his family have been wine-makers since 1640. He also makes a Mercurey.

BOURGOGNE AC. r.w
Nature et Progrès. 20,000 bottles p.a. 50-70 Hl/hectare
Guy Chaumont, St. Désert, 71390 Buxy, SAONE ET LOIRE

FRANCE – BURGUNDY

Guy Chaumont decided to use organic methods in 1965 following a "decision of conscience relative to a problem of health". More than that he does not say. He grows traditional Burgundy grapes with which he makes several other wines which are listed separately.

'82 r There were brown hues in the colour, interest in the nose; it was sweet but short, biscuity, lingering, but lacking generosity.

'83 r This too had brown hues but had a better nose. The fruit was maybe a bit thin and there was a hard earthy finish which suggested too much tannin.

'84 r Ripe, forthcoming and rooty on the nose, this was light, dry and volatile in the mouth and was generally considered attractive; it lost points on a lack of length.

'85 w The colour of this wine was "off"; there was strawiness rather than brightness. Somebody commented on an aroma of cheap butter and another of a fruit-stone flavour but there was an unexpected harshness and insubstantial weight which all suggested the wine had aged prematurely.

BOURGOGNE AC. r
Fédération Nationale d'Agriculture Biologique. 30-40,000 bottles p.a. 40-45 Hl/hectare
Alain, Janine et Pierre Guillot, Domaine des Vignes du Maynes, Cruzilles-en-Maconnais, 71260 Lugny. SAONE ET LOIRE. tel 85 33 20 15

They have been using organic methods here since 1954 but since no particular method was properly defined they developed their own system and are now with the Fédération Nationale d'Agriculture Biologique in Paris. Apart from the standard "clean" composts they encourage ladybirds, to eat other insects, and only use sulphur three or four times a year against mildew and odium and never use sulphur dioxide afterwards. They do in fact claim to be the oldest organic wine-growers and consider themselves to be setting the trend in agriculture for the next millennium. They grow Gamay, Pinot

Noir and Chardonnay and make a white and pink sparkler as well as the Macons listed elsewhere.

BOURGOGNE AC. r.w
Nature et Progrès. 3-10,000 bottles p.a. 20-42 Hl/hectare
Jean Javillier, 6 Rue Charles Giraud, 21190 Meursault, COTE D'OR. tel 80 21 24 61

Jean Javillier has been making wine since 1972 and is interested in natural medicine as well as natural wine. 1986 was a good year for him and not only weatherwise; with compost made by himself he enormously increased his yield and he has high hopes for the future. His other wines are listed elsewhere.

'85 w Flecked with gold and green, this wine had a lightly spiced, reserved nose and on the palate tasted of apples, soft fruit and cinnamon, although we thought it a little insipid.

BOURGOGNE AC. r
Alain Verdet, Arcenant, 21700 Nuits-St-Georges, COTE D'OR

'84 r This had warm orangey tones with a penetrating Pinot nose which reminded us of ginger and fish (not unpleasantly).

In the mouth there was a refreshing astringency and hints of violets and lychees but it was perhaps a little lacking in fruit.

FRANCE – BURGUNDY

BOURGOGNE ALIGOTE AC. w
Nature et Progrès. 3-10,000 bottles p.a. 20-42 Hl/hectare
Jean Javillier, 6 Rue Charles Giraud, 21190 Meursault, COTE D'OR. tel 80 21 24 61

'85 This had quite a deep colour with a complex nose of apples, spice and greenery. It was lemony, tart and refreshing, was well balanced with a long aftertaste and more complex than expected. Why replant with Chardonnay?

BOURGOGNE ALIGOTE AC. w
Alain Verdet, Arcenant, 21700 Nuits-St-Georges, COTE D'OR

BOURGOGNE-HAUTES CÔTES DE NUITS AC. r.w.
Alain Verdet, Arcenant, 21700 Nuits-St-Georges, COTE D'OR

'82 r With an orange hue, this had a lovely Burgundy nose and hints of smoke and cherries. It was beautifully balanced with rich soft fruit, a touch of oak and a satisfying complexity; there was a residual richness on the finish and we all thought it was drinking perfectly.

Bourgogne Passetoutgrain AC. r
Nature et Progrès. 15,000 bottles p.a. 40-60 Hl/hectare
Pierre d'Heilly et Martine Huberdeau, Cercot-Moroges, 71390 Buxy, SAONE ET LOIRE. tel 85 47 95 27

Pierre d'Heilly and Martine Huberdeau have backgrounds in environmental health, chemistry, biology, ecology and ethology and in 1978 the opportunity arose to establish themselves on a small family estate and put their training into practice in viticulture. They not only learned the trade with the local wine producers but also attended a training course organised by the local Chamber of Agriculture. Their estate was run down as far as vines were concerned but they have been replanting plot by plot and now have three hectares, two and a half of which are producing. They grow Pinot Noir, Aligote, Chardonnay and Gamay, the last being blended with the Pinot Noir to make the Passetoutgrain. The bulk of their production is Bourgogne red and Aligote.

Bourgogne Passetoutgrain AC. r
Fédération Nationale d'Agriculture Biologique. 30-40,000 bottles p.a. 40-50 Hl/hectare
Alain, Janine et Pierrre Guillot, Domaine des Vignes du Maynes, Cruzilles-en-Maconnais, 71260 Lugny, SAONE ET LOIRE. tel 85 33 20 15

Château de Boisfranc AC. Beaujolais Supérieur. r
Nature et Progrès. 40,000 bottles p.a. 40-66 Hl/hectare
Thierry Doat, Domaine de Boisfranc, 69640 Jarnioux, RHONE. tel 74 68 20 9l

Monsieur Doat has five hectares of vineyard and makes both Beaujolais and Nouveau. He likes a short fermentation, five to six days, to get more fruit than tannin, and to this end he heats his cellars which also speeds up the malo-lactic fermentation. The wine is then chilled to precipitate the solids and preserve the colour. He does not use sulphur in the vineyards or during the vinification but uses a little before bottling, one to two grammes per hectolitre.

FRANCE – BURGUNDY

CÔTES DE BEAUNE AC. r.w.
Biodynamie/Nature et Progrès. 5,000 bottles p.a. 45 Hl/hectare
Pierrette et Jean-Claude Rateau, Chemin des Mariages, 21200 Beaune, COTE D'OR. tel 80 22 52 54

'85 r A ripe Pinot nose that took some time to develop led on to a nice fruity flavour with raspberries predominating.

CRÉMANT DE BOURGOGNE AC. w.rosé
Alain Verdet, Arcenant, 21700 Nuits-St-Georges, COTE D'OR

NV w This had a deep colour although the mousse was a little disappointing and the floral bouquet reminded us of rosewater, peaches and cider apples. The flavour was full but elegant and the wine as a whole was well liked.

NV rosé This wine was a nice straw pink colour and had a peachy, yeasty nose. With no strong characteristics, the tasters found it refreshing, drinkable and flavoursome.

DOMAINE DE MALLEVAL AC. BEAUJOLAIS VILLAGES. r
Victor Michon

'83 Light red in colour and going at the rim, this had a concentrated fruity, tarry nose that some thought Pinot-ish.

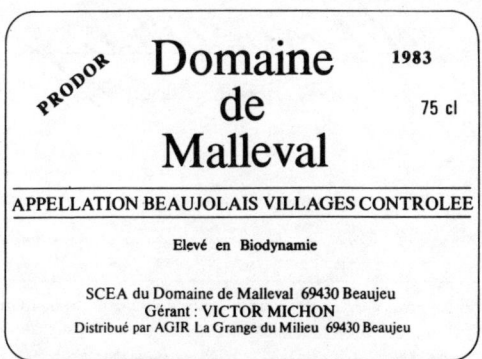

There was a good acidity but little mellow fruit and could well have been a little over the top. There was an uncanny undertone of black olives.

THE ORGANIC WINE GUIDE

HAUTES CÔTES DE BEAUNE AC r
Nature et Progrès
Jean Musso, Dracy-les-Couches, SAONE ET LOIRE

'83 Everybody agreed on the attractive fruity nose citing tayberries and other soft fruit, and they also agreed that the taste was too astringent (good stable, bad horse, thought one taster).

MACON AC. r.w
Fédération Nationale d'Agriculture Biologique. 30-40,000 bottles p.a. 40-45 Hl/hectare
Alain, Janine et Pierre Guillot, Domaine des Vignes du Maynes, Cruzilles-en-Maconnais, 71260 Lugny, SAONE ET LOIRE. tel 85 33 20 15

This family also make a red Burgundy. See notes.

MERCUREY AC. r
André Chaumont, St Jean de Vaux, 71640 Givry, SAONE ET LOIRE

'85 The nose on this was just stirring and was still a bit dumb but the wine was well-knit and obviously needs some time.

FRANCE – BURGUNDY

'84 This had light but good fruit, was forthcoming with some finesse and was considered "good to drink".

'83 A good amber colour led on to a tannic rather than fruity nose that reminded one taster of cooked cauliflower. It was well developed and flavourful with a touch of complexity and was generally enjoyed.

'82 This had an intense peppery nose and an unbalanced flavour of crushed pips and cocoa-butter.

MERCUREY AC. r
Nature et Progrès. 20,000 bottles p.a. 50-60 Hl/hectare
Guy Chaumont, St Désert, 71390 Buxy, SAONE ET LOIRE.

MERCUREY AC. r
Hubert Garrey, Saint-Martin-sous-Montaigue, 71640 Givry, SAONE ET LOIRE

Hubert Garrey uses his own organic system which incorporates some natural fungicides, a little Bordeaux mixture, sulphur and potassium permanganate plus a Lemaire-Boucher based fertiliser and compost. Primarily he makes organic wine because it is safe for the grower, it reduces cost, it grows better vines and it ensures the most natural product possible. Secondly because it is a product that is more and more in demand. He uses a bain-marie system to heat the fermentation vats and matures the wine in oak casks for two years before bottling. He also makes a red Burgundy.

MEURSAULT AC. w
Nature et Progrès. 3-10,000 bottles p.a. 20-42 Hl/hectare
Jean Javillier, 6 Rue Charles Giraud, 21190 Meursault, COTE D'OR

PULIGNY-MONTRACHET AC. w
Biodynamie/Nature et Progrès. 2,000 bottles p.a. 45 Hl/hectare
Pierrette et Jean-Claude Rateau, Chemin des Mariages, 21200 Beaune, COTE D'OR. tel 80 22 52 54

THE ORGANIC WINE GUIDE

Volnay Santenots AC. r
Nature et Progrès. 3-10,000 bottles p.a. 20-42 Hl/hectare
Jean Javillier, 6 Rue Charles Giraud, 21190 Meursault, COTE D'OR. tel 80 21 24 61

The most expensive of his wines, it is also the smallest production.

CHAMPAGNE

Lying to the north-east of Paris, Champagne is the most northerly wine-growing region in France and this goes a long way in explaining its particular nature. Due to the cool climate fermentation did not always completely finish and in the spring would start up again, causing a slight fizziness or petillance; the casks used to transport the wine were often known to fizz up.

The first major development in the creation of the modern Champagne was carried out by Dom Pérignon, cellar master of the abbey of Hautvilliers, when he started tying on the corks to secure the fizz in the bottle. He was also a master blender, which is also an important factor in the drink.

At the beginning of the 19th century the widow Clicquot invented a wooden frame which held the bottles upside down; the bottles were twisted every day and the sediment resulting from the second fermentation gathered on the cork – a technique known as "remuage". The cork was removed ("dégorgement"), the wine containing the sediment discarded, and the bottle was topped up with wine and recorked. In 1884 Raymond Abbèle improved on this technique by inserting the neck of the bottle in a very cold brine mixture, freezing the sediment solution, and again this was removed, the bottle topped up and recorked. Today the technique is much the same although technology has taken over some of the more labour-intensive areas.

Champagne is a white wine made mostly from black grapes: the Pinot Noir, the Pinot Meunière and the Chardonnay. Great care is taken not to let the unfermented grape juice pick up any colour from the black grape skins. The must is fermented as a standard white wine and then the wine intended

FRANCE – CHAMPAGNE

for the non-vintage version is blended; this can involve up to 30 different wines from different vintages all contributing to the desired house style. Sugar and yeast are added to the bottle and the second fermentation commences. When this is complete the sediment is removed and the bottle is topped up with a mixture of sugar and wine, called the "dosage", which determines the sweetness of the wine. It is generally considered that without this the wine is too dry; it can also cover up any thinness. Vintage champagne is also blended from grapes from different vineyards but they must come from the same year. Blanc de Blanc Champagne is made solely from the Chardonnay and rosé Champagne gets its colour from the addition of red wine.

THE ORGANIC WINE GUIDE

CHAMPAGNE AC. w
Nature et Progrès
José Ardinat, Rue de la Gallicheterie, 51700 VANDIÈRES. tel 26 50 36 07

NV Fine, warm, yellow in colour, this had crisp biscuity flavours with fresh light gooseberry fruit.

CHAMPAGNE AC. w
André et Jacques Beaufort, 1 Rue de Vandemanges, 5110 Ambonnay, MARNE

They also make a white and red vin de table.

CHAMPAGNE AC. w
Serge Faust, Vandières, 51700 Dormans, MARNE

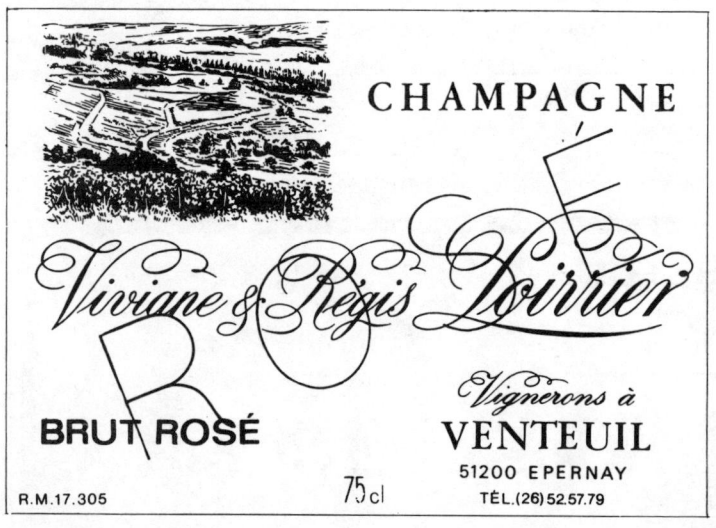

CHAMPAGNE AC. w
Roger Fransoret, Ferme d'Alencourt, Mancy, 51200 Épernay, MARNE. tel 26 59 70 68

A Côteaux Champenois white and red is also made.

FRANCE – LOIRE

CHAMPAGNE AC. w
Thomas Hussent, Oger, 51190 Avize, MARNE

CHAMPAGNE AC. w
Georges Laval, Cumières, 51200 Épernay, MARNE

CHAMPAGNE AC. w
Paul Letuvée, 624 Avenue de Gl. Leclerc, 51200 Dizy, MARNE

CHAMPAGNE AC. w. rosé
Nature et Progrès. 6,000 bottles p.a.
Viviane et Régis Poirrier, 1 Rue d'Église, Venteuil, 51200 Épernay, MARNE. tel 26 58 49 61

Régis and Viviane Poirrier have been using organic methods since 1969.

NV rosé A lovely, pale, silky pink, with a yeasty nose, plenty of tiny bubbles and a full, almost mellow, fruity flavour.

CHAMPAGNE AC. w
Yves Ruffin, Avenay Val d'Or, 51160 Ay, MARNE

An Ambonnay red is also made.

THE LOIRE

Running from the Massif Central to the Atlantic, the Loire passes through a variety of landscapes and micro-climates but still manages to maintain its own unique character. This can in part be explained by its northern position which gives an acidity to balance the fruit and, with one or two exceptions, not an excessive amount of alcohol. Famous not only for its vineyards, most people will think of the High Renaissance châteaux and gastronomes will know it as the "Garden of France".

Sauvignon is the grape predominant at the head of the Loire where it is turned into the trendsetting wines of Sancerre and Pouilly Fumé; gunflint is often used to describe their particular charm, but as has already been pointed out by other writers, how many of us are acquainted with gunflint?

Coming downstream, we arrive at Touraine where the two principal red wines are Chinon and Bourgueil, made from Cabernet Franc, and are normally drunk young but can mature up to five to seven years. The most famous white wine is Vouvray, made from the Chenin Blanc grape, and it can be dry, sweet or a sparkler. For the sweet Vouvrays noble rot is encouraged and failing that the grapes are allowed to become overripe in the autumn sun. An up-and-coming addition to the wines of the region is Touraine Sauvignon, remarkably fresh and reasonably priced.

Anjou was most well known for the region's rosé. However, I suspect in Britain the most-drunk Loire rosé wine now is the sparkling Saumur. Chenin Blanc is again the predominant white wine grape, making both crisp dry and luscious sweet wines of great character. It must be said, though, that they can be a bit stinky when young. Cabernet Franc is used for the rosés as well as the reds.

The automatic choice of a lot of people when they order a fish course in a restaurant will be Muscadet, and it is around the mouth of the Loire that this wine is made. The Melon de Bourgogne grape is used and it can be bottled in two different ways. The traditional, and to my mind the best, way is to leave the fermented must in the cask without racking it onthe lees (the label will say "sur lie") and bottling it the following spring. This results in a weightier, more flavoursome, wine that may have a slight sparkle due to a light second fermentation. It is less trouble just to rack and fine the wine to give a lighter but still delicious wine that really does go well with all seafood, unless it is very heavily sauced.

ANJOU AC. w
Yves Freulon, Dreuille, 49380 Champ sur Layon. MAINE ET LOIRE. tel 41 78 87 03

NV This one caused a division in the tasting ranks; on one side people commented "nice Chenin nose" and "typical" whereas others thought the nose "very powerful glue", "rotten" and "foully fishy". The same alliterative soul also said "flavourless flab fouls it up"; however, two members of the trade thought it "dry, crisp and racy" and another "good balance and length but too young". Take your pick.

ANJOU AC. r
Yves Freulon, Dreuille, 49380 Champ sur Layon, MAINE ET LOIRE. tel 41 78 87 03

'85 In general this was considered to have a reasonable nose with a hint of anise and again "reasonable" was used to describe the fruit. However, it had no start and a tart finish. The mention of Cabernet on the label refers to Cabernet Franc rather than Sauvignon.

ANJOU AC. r
Terre et Vie. 30-60 Hl/hectare
J. Nouteau-Cérisier, "Le Verger", 49380 Faye-d'Anjou, MAINE ET LOIRE. tel 41 54 31 40

Monsieur Nouteau-Cérisier considers Terre et Vie to be the only méthode biologique that has a quality contract which is strictly supervised. The family has been making wine for several generations, but after several "accidents" with their vines and wines they decided to return to more natural methods. They produce several other wines which are mentioned in the text.

BLANC CÔTEAUX DU LAYON AC. w
J. Nouteau-Cérisier. "Le Verger", 49380 Faye-d'Anjou, MAINE ET LOIRE. tel 41 54 31 40

BLANC CÔTEAUX DU VILLAGE FAYE AC. w
J. Nouteau-Cérisier. "Le Verger", 49380 Faye-d'Anjou, MAINE ET LOIRE. tel 41 54 31 40

BOURGUEIL AC. r
Christian Georget, La Brosse Touvois, 37140 Bourgueil, INDRE ET LOIRE

Made from the Cabernet Franc grape in certain years, given enough tannin these wines can keep for up to ten years.

THE ORGANIC WINE GUIDE

Cabernet d'Anjou-Domaine de Dreuille AC. rosé
Yves Freulon, Dreuille, 49380 Champ sur Layon, MAINE ET LOIRE. tel 41 78 87 03

'85 This was a delicate pink colour with a sharp clean nose that belied the soft strawberry fruit. An initial sweetness seemed to disappear after a while.

Cabernet d'Anjou AC. rosé
Terre et Vie
J. Nouteau-Cérisier, "Le Verger", 49380 Faye-d'Anjou, MAINE ET LOIRE. tel 41 54 31 40

Cépage Grolleau Gris AC. w
J. Nouteau-Cérisier. "Le Verger", 49380 Faye-d'Anjou, MAINE ET LOIRE. tel 41 54 31 40

Made from a grape that is virtually unique to the Loire Valley, especially Touraine, this variety produces a dark white wine with occasional hints of rosiness.

Clos Rougeard AC. Saumur. r
Ch. et F. Foucault, Clos Rougeard, 15 Rue de l'Église, 49560 Chace, MAINE ET LOIRE

A rare red wine from this are renowned for its fizzy whites.

Côteaux du Layon-moelleux AC. w
Yves Freulon, Dreuille, 49380 Champ sur Layon, MAINE ET LOIRE. tel 41 78 87 03

'85 Pale yellow in colour, this wine had a lanolin nose with an acidic edge; on the palate it was quite sweet but it was balanced by good acidity and reminded somebody of lemon frangipane.

Domaine des Dorices, Muscadet de Sèvres et Maine AC. w
L. Bouillault et Fils, Vallet, LOIRE-ATLANTIQUE

'85 Very pale in colour, words like pungent, rotten, gooseberry, grapy, yeasty and fully characteristic came up in the tasting notes. Made sur lie, it had above-average fruit, was fuller than expected and had a dry, clean, acidic finish with no decline into tartness.

FRANCE – LOIRE

MUSACDET DE SÈVRES ET MAINE AC. w
Henri Antier et Fils, La Bodinière Tillières, 49230 Montfaucon, MAINE ET LOIRE

Red, white and rosé are also made.

MUSCADET DE SÈVRES ET MAINE AC. w
Terre et Vie. 75,000 bottles p.a. 30-70 Hl/hectare
Guy Bossard, La Bretonnière, 44430 Le Landreau, MAINE ET LOIRE

The Bossards have been making wine for five generations and have been using the Terre et Vie standards since 1972 and give

THE ORGANIC WINE GUIDE

safeguarding the soil, improving the flavour of the wine and preserving the health of their customers as their reasons. They use both horse and tractor for accurate cultivation and the grapes are still picked by hand. They also make wine from the Gros Plant (a popular white grape at the mouth of the Loire) and from the Cabernet Franc as well as plain grape juice.

'85 A pale yellow with decided petillance, this was a dry, grapy wine with balanced fruit, fresh, clean lemons predominating. It was voted top in a recent *Which? Wine Monthly* tasting of Muscadets.

ROSÉ D'ANJOU AC. rosé
J. Nouteau-Cérisier. "Le Verger", 49380 Faye-d'Anjou, MAINE ET LOIRE. tel 41 54 31 40

SANCERRE AC. r.w.rosé
Terre et Océan
Nicole et Christian Dauny, Champtin, Crézancy en Sancerre, 18300 Sancerre, CHER. tel 48 79 05 75

Becoming popular in London restaurants; one shipper of this wine claims that some elderly ladies drink one bottle of this

instead of a quarter bottle of Perrier. Wisdom comes with age.

'86 w Lime and lychees on the nose, carrying into the mouth where more fruits and good fresh acidity await. Much less austere than expected.

'86 r Light in colour and weight, this is nevertheless an attractive, fruity mouthful with a pleasing residual tartness. Carefree summer drinking.

'86 rosé A verdant nose contrasts the colour but a lemony acidity dominates the taste and aftertaste.

SAUMUR AC. w
Nature et Progrès. 20-30,000 bottles p.a. 50-60 Hl/hectare
Gérard Leroux, Les Verchers sur Layon, 49700 Doue-La-Fontane, MAINE ET LOIRE. tel 41 59 17 59

Gérard Leroux had been having problems with his farm animals and after tests decided to clean up his fields and vineyards, and adopted the Lamaire-Boucher method in 1964, changing to Nature et Progrès in 1976. He uses Chenin Blanc for his Saumur but also grows Cabernet Franc, Cabernet

Sauvignon, and Groslot or Grolleau (a high yielder peculiar to the Loire) from which he makes Anjou Blanc, Côteaux du Layon, Anjou Rouge and a Rosé d'Anjou.

NV With a definitely yeasty nose, the bottle we tasted almost broke a window when the cork shot out unexpectedly. A lovely straw colour with tiny bubbles, it was dry and toasted with a good bitter finish. Altogether a strong wine.

SAUMUR AC. w
Émile Courtilleau, Savoie, Berrie, 86120 Les Trois Moutiers, VIENNE.

THE MIDI AND THE SOUTH-WEST

The history of wine in the south of France stretches as far back as the eighth century BC when the Greeks developed vineyards in the Languedoc. The Romans subsequently developed this so successfully and the competition with Italian wine became so great that the Emperor Domitian ordered the destruction of half the vineyards in AD92. The Emperor Probus lifted the restrictions in AD270 and the area again was developed, this time by the Visigoths, but the Saracens soon put a stop to this. The area was replanted by the monasteries during the ninth century and with the increase of trade, prosperity and transport during the 17th, 18th and 19th centuries the region was pouring out wine in great quantities, if not of great quality. This could still be said to be the case but since the 1950s certain winemakers, co-operatives and regions have been making serious efforts to increase quality to reach the increasing critical demands of the world market.

In the south-west the principal areas of interest are Cahors, Gaillac, Bergerac and, perhaps the more familiar of pudding wines, Monbazillac. In the Midi itself big efforts have been made to replant with more interesting grape varieties; at the moment Carignan, Cinsault, Grenache, Mourvèdre and Syrah are predominant with a little Cabernet Sauvignon and Merlot. The carbonic maceration technique has also been found useful

FRANCE – MIDI AND SOUTH-WEST

in extracting more fruit to compensate for the traditional lack of character. The areas of interest here are the Minervois, Corbières, Costières du Gard, Côtes du Roussillon and Côtes du Roussillon-Village. Further to the east, Provence is notorious for its alcoholic rosés. However, certain winemakers are getting terrific amounts of attention for their organically grown wines, e.g. Monsieur Durrbach on a rocky outcrop in the Côteaux de Baux en Provence for his Domaine de Trevallon.

ALBARIC ACC. r
Nature et Progrès
Alain and Hoirie Albaric, Domaine de L'Isle de Sables, Fourques, 13200 Arles, BOUCHES DU RHONE. tel 90 96 38 25

NV This one really split opinion; one faction thought it had an attractive caramel nose, good fruit and a lovely spicy finish, whereas the others were reminded of cherry cough medicine and thought it light, metallic, tinny and artificial.

BLANQUETTE DE LIMOUX AC. w
Nature et Progrès. 13,000 bottles p.a. 40 Hl/hectare
Jean-Claude Beirieu, Roquetaillade, 11300 Limoux. tel 68 31 60 71

Some consider that the sparkling wines of Limoux predate those of Champagne by a hundred years. This may be so but now the majority of wine is made by the Champagne method. Not this one, though. Monsieur Beirieu makes his wine by the traditional method. The must is fermented in the normal way but leaving a residual sugar. It is then bottled in the spring at just the moment when the spontaneous second fermentation starts. This results not only in a sparkle but also a sediment in the bottle – a perfectly normal occurrence which does not affect the taste of the wine. Monsieur Beirieu has been making organic wine since 1981 and has a great respect for the tradition of the master vignerons of the area as well as the health of the soil and his fellow man.

'85 There was not as much pressure as a Champagne type but this was to be expected. There was a lovely aroma of elderflowers and peaches and the taste was remarkably refreshing rather than serious.

BLANQUETTE DE LIMOUX AC w
Nature et Progrès
GAEC la Solana, Festes, 11300 Limoux. tel 68 31 13 11

BOUCHARDON. VIN DE TABLE. r.w
Nature et Progrès
Bouchardon S.N.C., 03 Hyds, ALLIERS. tel 70 64 38 07

This commune of 380 inhabitants has been producing wine under the control of Nature et Progrès for 15 years and exports it to seven European countries as well as the USA.

NV Vibrant purple red in colour, this went for the eyes and seemed chemically unnatural. There was a sick taste and nobody would or could swallow it. Overenthusiastic sales led to a drop in quality and some existing shippers are not too happy with the situation.

CARBARDÈS. VDQS. r
Lemaire-Boucher. 2,000 bottles p.a. 50 Hl/hectare
Jean-Claude et Annie Loupia, Les Albarels de Pennautier, 11000 CARCASSONNE. tel 68 24 91 77.

The Loupias have been using organic methods since 1974 and are enthusiastic promoters of their wines and beliefs. They receive students from a number of countries such as France, England and Poland to make known that these methods can have very positive results. They also organise a fair of biological produce every June with the help of the Carcassonne Council and the local Chamber of Trade and Industry.

'85 This had an attractive deep colour and initially a slightly farmyardy nose. Nice soft Merlot fruit predominated and there was a lingering vinous follow-on.

FRANCE – MIDI AND SOUTH-WEST

CHARDONNAY. VIN DE PAYS D'OC. w
Listel
'83 This wine had a slight sparkle and a very faint Chardonnay nose. However, it had a firm, stony, lemony taste if lacking in character and was probably a bit old.

CHÂTEAU LE BARRADIS AC MONBAZILLAC AND BERGERAC. r.w. rosé
Nature et Progrès. 80-100,000 bottles white p.a., 30-50,000 bottles red p.a. 26 Hl/hectare white, 50 Hl/hectare.
Jacques-Victor Mornai (M et Mme Labasse-Gazzini), Château le Barradis, 24240 Sigoules, Monbazillac, DORDOGNE. tel 53 58 30 01

Jacques-Victor makes a number of wines at Château le Barradis, the sweet white Monbazillac, a non-appellation

sparkler called Reserve Saint Christophe, and a red, white and rosé Bergerac. He has been making wine personally since 1967 and used the Lemaire-Boucher method from 1968 until he changed to Nature et Progrès in 1981; he had heard a lot about the progress to be made using chemicals but considered that real progress lay in a different direction. He uses Semillon, Sauvignon and Muscadelle for his whites and Merlot and Cabernet Sauvignon for the reds. As part of his publicity hand-out he includes extracts from a *Guide diétetique et médicamenteux des vins* by a Doctor Maury which recommends Monbazillac for tired stomachs, dyspepsia and people who have lost their appetites, and Bergerac Blanc for obesity; you can tell the French care for their stomachs.

'83 An oaty, shortbread aroma led on to a wine with lots of flavour and character that several thought delicious. There was a touch of bitterness on the aftertaste and one taster thought it was getting old quickly.

CHÂTEAU STE. ANNE. AC CÔTES DE PROVENCE, AC BANDOL.
r.w
François Dutheil de la Rochère, Château Ste. Anne, 83330 Ste. Anne d'Évenos, VAR. tel 94 90 35 40

The Bandol is a dark tanniny wine for laying down made from the Mourvèdre, Cinsault and Grenache grape, whereas the white Côtes de Provence is lighter and made for more immediate consumption.

CHÂTEAU VIGNELAURE. VDQS CÔTE AUX D'AIX EN PROVENCE.
r
Georges Brunet, Château Vignelaure, 83560 Rians, VAR. tel 94 80 31 93

Famous for restoring Château La Lagune in the Médoc, Georges Brunet moved to Provence in the 1960s and planted Cabernet Sauvignon to spruce up the local grapes. There is nothing rustic about this wine, which will benefit from keeping; like one or two other wines from this region it is much classier than the VDQS appellation suggests.

CLOS MIREILLE. VDQS CÔTE DE PROVENCE. w
Henri Ott, 83250 La Londe les Maures. VAR

Made close to the sea, this white comes in a strangely shaped bottle. The Otts also make a wine called Les Borrels.

CÔTE AUX DE LANGUEDOC AC. r
Nature et Progrès. 16,000 bottles p.a. 72 Hl/hectare
Simone Couderc, 32 Rue du Conseil Général, 34320 Neffies, HÉRAULT. tel 67 24 62 28

Simone Couderc has been making wine all her life, as did her parents before her. Still using a horse, she grows Grenache, Syrah and Carignan and uses the carbonic maceration technique to get as much fruit as possible for the red wine; it is then matured in oak casks for six months or more.

CÔTEAUX DE LA CITÉ DE CARCASSONNE. VINS DE PAYS. r.w.
Lemaire-Boucher. 8,000 bottles p.a. 50 Hl/hectare.
Jean-Claude et Annie Loupia, Les Albarels de Pennautier, 11000 CARCASSONNE. tel 68 24 91 77.

NV w With a yeasty, sherbety nose this wine seemed a bit unbalanced but had a pleasant tart aftertaste.

NV r Very light cherry in colour this had a distinctly peppery taste which quietened down into a clean fruity aftertaste.

CRU DES VALADES-CANTÉGREL. AC BERGERAC. r
Jean Guiraud, Les Valades, 24560 Issigeac, DORDOGNE.

DOMAINE DE CLAIRAC. VIN DE PAYS DE L'HÉRAULT. r.w
Lemaire-Boucher. 150,000 bottles p.a. 80 Hl/hectare
GFA de Clairac, 34370 Cazouls les Béziers, HÉRAULT. tel 67 90 55 62

Problems with personal health as a result of working with chemical products decided Monsieur Joubio on the organic course and he has been making wine since 1960. They plant Syrah, Grenache, Cinsault and Carignan for the vins de pays and use oak barrels for maturation.

THE ORGANIC WINE GUIDE

Joubio NV This had a youthful, medium colour and a nose of sweet plums and petrol. Someone mentioned a good nose hidden by a rubber mask. On the palate it seemed a little unbalanced with a jamminess and mineral undertones, a typical Hérault.

Cêpage Cabernet '84 "High toned" and "medicinal" were used to describe the nose of the wine. However, it tasted better than expected although a touch metallic. It became more Cabernet-like with the aftertaste.

Cêpage Syrah '85 This had a good warm colour and had a slightly medicinal whiff; dry and youthful but drinking now. It had a light fruit finish.

DOMAINE DE GRESSAC. VINS DE PAYS DES CÔTEAUX DE CÈZE. r.w.rosé
Lemaire-Boucher. 20-30,000 bottles p.a. 50 Hl/hectare
Arlette et Lucien Bondurand, Verfeuil, 30630 Goudargues, GARD. tel 66 72 90 36

The Bondurands have been using the Lemaire-Boucher method since 1960 in their vineyards among the wooded hills of the Cèze valley next to the Rhône. They make their wine in the traditional way without stalking or added yeast and using a hydraulic wine press. They make a number of wines, among them the red Cuvée de Court; this is made from 70% Grenache and 30% Mourvèdre and the grape-picking is organised so that the two grapes can ferment together as opposed to the common method of assembling wines afterwards. Another red called Les Abeilles, a rosé and a white are also made.

Cuvée de Court '85 A dark purply wine with nice fruit and acidity which evoked the comment "stewed raspberry" from one taster. A bitter aftertaste suggests it might improve over a year or two.

DOMAINE DE LA CHAUME. VDQS CÔTEAUX DE PIERREVERT. r
Nature et Progrès. 20,000 bottles p.a. 45 Hl/hectare
Jouannin-Cormier, La Chaume, 04860 Pierrevert, ALPES DE HAUTE PROVENCE. tel 92 87 57 51

They have only been making wine since 1978 in their vineyard in the heart of Haute Provence (average height 500 metres) but in 1986 they were awarded the gold medal at the Avignon wine fair. The grapes used are 60% Syrah, 20% Merlot and 20% Cabernet Sauvignon and they are fermented using the carbonic maceration method and the result is neither filtered nor fined but simply racked off. This is a wine to watch out for.

DOMAINE DE LA GAUTIÈRE. VIN DE PAYS DES CÔTEAUX DES BARONNIES. r. rosé
GAEC de la Gautière. La Penne-sur-Ouvèse, 26170 Buis-les-Baronnies, DROME. tel 75 28 09 58

A red and rosé produced by producers of organic herbs, honey, olives, cereals etc.

DOMAINE DE LANDUE. AC CÔTES DE PROVENCE. r
Nature et Progrès
Germain Arnaud, Domaine de Landue, 83210 Sollies Pont, VAR. tel 94 28 94 87

DOMAINE DE L'EAU SALÉE. VIN DE TABLE. r
Nature et Progrès
Richard Carbonnel, Domaine de l'Eau Salée, 83670 Barjols, PROVENCE. tel 94 77 04 15

DOMAINE DE L'ÎLE. AC LIMOUX, VINS DE PAYS DE L'AUDE. r.w
Lemaire-Boucher. 23,000 bottles white p.a., 25,000 bottles red p.a. 60 Hl/hectare
Ernest Bissa, Domaine de l'Île, 11260 Esperaza, AUDE. tel 68 74 07 97

This domaine is situated in the Haute Vallée de l'Aude and benefits from a micro-climate which is both Mediterranean and maritime; the grapes planted are Mauzac for the white Limoux (peculiar to the area), Carignan, Cinsault and Cabernet Sauvignon. The bulk of the production is the vin de pays red but they also produce a rosé, 9,000 bottles of Cabernet and two Blanquettes de Limoux, one by the "ancestrale" method and the other by méthode Champenoise.

THE ORGANIC WINE GUIDE

DOMAINE DE L'ÎLE. AC LIMOUX. VINS DE PAYS DE L'AUDE. r.w.rosé

NV rosé This was an attractive light rosé colour and its slightly stinky nose contrasted with a clean fruity taste. Attractive and not at all a heavy rosé.

NV r Purply pink in colour, clean light fruit predominated. There was perhaps a lack of acidity and tannin but overall it was considered an appealing wine.

DOMAINE DE L'ÎLE DES SABLES. VIN DE TABLE. r
Nature et Progrès
Hoirie Albaric, Fourques, 13200 Arles, BOUCHES DU RHONE. tel 90 96 38 25

DOMAINE DE MALARIC. VIN DE PAYS DE L'UZÈGE. r.rosé
Terre-Océan
GFA de Malaric, Pont des Charrettes, 30700 Uzes, GARD

NV Dull, pinky purple, this whiffed of sorbic acid, was dry and acidic in the mouth and prompted comments about chemistry lab.

DOMAINE DE RÉGUSSE. VDQS CÔTES DE PIERREVERT
Claude Dieudonné, Domaine de Régusse, 04860 Pierrevert, ALPES DE HAUTE PROVENCE. tel 92 72 30 44

DOMAINE DE ST. CRESCENT. VDQS CORBIÈRE. r.w.rosé
Nature et Progrès
Mme Edmond Hérail, Avenue de Gal Leclerc, 11100 Narbonne, AUDE. tel 68 32 06 96

Mme Hérail also makes vins du pays de l'Aude.

DOMAINE DE SNHILAC. VIN DE PAYS DU GARD
Louis Giraudet, Domaine de Snhilac, 30800 St Gilles, GARD

DOMAINE DE TREVALLON. VDQS CÔTE AUX DES BAUX EN PROVENCE. r

FRANCE – MIDI AND SOUTH-WEST

Éloi et Jacqueline Durrbach, 13150 St. Étienne-du-Grès,
BAUX EN PROVENCE

Championed recently by the American claret expert, Robert Parker, this is the most talked-about wine in this book. Éloi Durrbach abandoned a career in architecture and started planting Cabernet Sauvignon and Syrah on a rocky outcrop of the Baux in 1973. In the opinion of Robin Yapp, ". . . Éloi counts as a fanatic, demanding transcendence in his wines . . . and is achieving that lofty goal". I was first introduced to it by David Brown of La Potinière in Gullane and have been a fan ever since.

'84 With a deep black colour, the class of this wine hits you immediately. Big, rich and dry, there is excellent fruit, berries predominating, with a leanness underlying the ripeness. Top class.

DOMAINE DES NUETS. VDQS CÔTES DE PROVENCE
Depport, Domaine des Nuets, 83570 Cotignac, VAR

THE ORGANIC WINE GUIDE

DOMAINE DES PALATS. AC CORBIÈRES. r
Nature et Progrès. 4-7,000 bottles p.a. 30 Hl/hectare
Tim Sparham, Domaine des Palats, Fonjoncouse, 11360 Durban-Corbières, AUDE. tel 68 44 05 76

Tim Sparham has lived in France for the past 16 years and began as a vigneron in a co-op in a neighbouring community. He still has vines in that "commune" but for the last two years he has had his own vineyard, Domaine des Palats, which he sells separately. He does in fact produce two wines, one using the entire grape (stalks and all) and the other which is matured in oak casks. He nearly always uses the carbonic maceration method "for which we need a nicer-sounding description in French as in English". He uses Grenache Carignan, Maccabeo and Grenache Blanc grapes and belongs to the tasting committee of the "Cru Corbières".

Brigitte and Jean-Marc Étienne

DOMAINE DU BAS-DEFFENS. VDQS CÔTEAUX VARIOS. r
Nature et Progrès. 30,000 bottles p.a. 35 Hl/hectare
Jean-Marc Étienne, Pontèves, 83670 Barjols, VAR. tel 94 77 10 36

FRANCE – MIDI AND SOUTH-WEST

Jean-Marc Étienne and his wife Brigitte have been making wine near Barjols for 14 years and plant Grenache, Cinsault, Cabernet Sauvignon, Syrah and Merlot. He quickly states his reasons for making vin biologique as ecological and commercial conviction.

'84 There were differing opinions about this wine. Some thought it was round and had good fruit whereas some found it dry, acid and "pointed".

DOMAINE DU FUMAT. AC MONBAZILLAC AND BERGERAC. w
Pierre Barjou, 24240 Sigoules, DORDOGNE

DOMAINE GENDRE MARSALET. AC CÔTES DE BERGERAC. r
Terre et Vie. 50,000 bottles p.a. 50 Hl/hectare
René Monbouche, 24240 Monbazillac, DORDOGNE. tel 53 57 94 36

As a result of eczema caused by consuming chemically treated products René Monbouche has been using organic methods since 1969. He plants only Merlot.

'85 This had a deeper colour than expected and had a good nose of ripe fruit. There was a nice balance between fruit and acidity and would make ideal summer drinking.

Domaine Grand Bourry. VDQS Costière du Gard
Nature et Progrès
Jean-Claude Falleri, Domaine Grand Bourry, 30740 Le Cailar, GARD. tel 66 88 61 36

Domaine Richeaume. AC Côtes de Provence.
r.w.rosé
Henning Hoesch, 13114 Puyloubier, PROVENCE. tel 42 29 21 80

Lying at the foot of the mountain range St. Victoire the Richeaume estate has 60 acres of vineyards as well as wheatfields and pasture for sheep, the straw and manure of which fertilise the vineyard. The old Provençal farmhouse lies next to the modern winery which not only houses things like stainless steel vats but also stained glass and designer fittings. Mr Hoesch, a colleague of Éloi Durrbach of Domaine de Trevallon, makes a number of wines, the principal red being the Cuvée Tradition which is a blend of Grenache, Cinsault and Carignan; he also makes a Cêpage Syrah and Cêpage Cabernet which are predominantly of these grapes. The different grapes from different parts of the vineyard are carefully tasted before the annual making of the cuvée and they are then blended in oak barrels for up to two years. He also makes a rosé and a white.

'85 r Made from Grenache, Cinsault and Carignan, this wine was full of fresh fruit and some style; the astringent aftertaste would suggest it could keep and improve.

Domaine St. André de Figuière. AC Côtes de Provence
Connesin Père et Fils, GFA Domaine St. André de Figuière, 83250 La Londe, VAR

Domaine St. Cyriaque. Vins de Pays and VDQS.
r.w.rosé
Nature et Progrès. 100,000 bottles p.a. 40-45 Hl/hectare
Claude Courtois, Route de Bras, 83143 Le Val, VAR. tel 94 86 44 16

FRANCE – MIDI AND SOUTH-WEST

Named after the patron saint of the village, the Domaine covers about 100 acres, half of which is vineyard; it is situated about 50 miles from the Mediterranean on a chalky clay soil at an altitude of 300 metres. Their white wines are made from Sauvignon, Semillon and Ugni Blanc and the rosés from Carignan, Grenache and Cinsault; both of these are vinified at low temperature to preserve flavour and bouquet. The Domaine St. Cyriaque is made with Carignan and Grenache using the carbonic maceration technique and the Cuvée St. Cyriaque is made from Syrah and Grenache and matured in oak casks.

'86 white With pale but attractive hues, this wine had a light herby nose with an undertone of old apples; it was flavoursome if a little clumsy and someone thought it overripe.

'86 red A healthy youthful colour and an up-front nose of hyacinths and musk led on to a bright, ripe taste of strawberries with something metallic. Good summer lunchtime drinking.

'85 Cuvée red Lots of purple and a Rhône-like nose introduced this wine; it was chalky, with attractive bite and fruit but one dissenter found it insubstantial and unclean.

LISTEL-ROUGE ROUBIS. VIN DE TABLE. r

NV Purply red in colour, the dominant flavours were round fruit, rough caramel and tannin.

LITENIS. VIN DE TABLE. r
Nature et Progrès. 15,000 bottles p.a. 40 Hl/hectare
Claude Destand, Cave de Litenis, 34150 St. Jean de Fos, HÉRAULT. tel 67 57 41 37

Claude Destand is keen to emphasise that his wine is made to be tannic because among the resulting tannins there are "procyanidines" which help prevent arteriosclerosis and purify the blood of cholesterol. To this end he uses the carbonic maceration technique to ferment the wine from eight to twelve days. He blends Grenache, Carignan, Syrah, Alicante and Merlot.

LOU CANTARIO. VIN DE PAYS DE L'HÉRAULT. r
Nature et Progrès
Guy Cros, 34980 La Caunette, HÉRAULT

NV Attractive purply red in colour, this wine had a nondescript nose but was well balanced and had attractive youthful fruit.

MAS DE GOURGONNIER. AC CÔTEAUX D'AIX EN PROVENCE LES BAUX. r.w.rosé
Nature et Progrès. 200,000 bottles p.a. 40-50 Hl/hectare
Nicolas Cartier, 13890 Mouries, BOUCHES DU RHONE

Apart from respect for nature and tradition, Nic Cartier has been making wine for 20 years because of his attitude to work and to life in general. He makes a white, red and rosé and uses Grenache, Syrah, Cabernet Sauvignon, Cinsault, Sauvignon and Ugni Blanc.

NV rosé One or two tasters found sulphur and toilet chemicals on first approach and thought that both bottles must be bad. On the other hand one or two thought it light and fruity, well balanced and lingering. One cynic commented that it could be an acquired taste.

'85 r A bit unclean on the nose although there was some pleasing complexity; jammy and Rhône-like, it was not unpleasant in the mouth.

'83 r Comments on the nose varied from ripe farmyardy to glucose lollipops. Peppery in taste, there was perhaps too little fruit and there was an acidic aftertaste.

FRANCE – MIDI AND SOUTH-WEST

MAS MADAGASCAR. VIN DE PAYS DU GARD. r
Nature et Progrès. 500 Hl.70 Hl/hectare
Jean-Paul Cabanis, 30640 Beauvoisin, GARD. tel 66 88 78 33

Jean-Paul Cabanis cites his reasons for making wine as interesting work, producing a quality wine and correct remuneration. He has been in business for four years and as yet only sells in bulk.

MINERVOIS. VDQS. r
Nature et Progrès
Guy Cros, 2 Boulevard de la République, 34420 Villeneuve Les Béziers, HÉRAULT. tel 67 32 17 05

A vin de pays de l'Hérault is also made.

QUOTIDIANUS. VIN DE TABLE. r
Terre-Océan
GFA de Malaric, Pont des Charrettes, Uzes, GARD

NV This wine was lurid pinky red and smelled of burnt rubber and medicine. One taster thought it nervy and dry and drinkable, just. Others found it completely unapproachable.

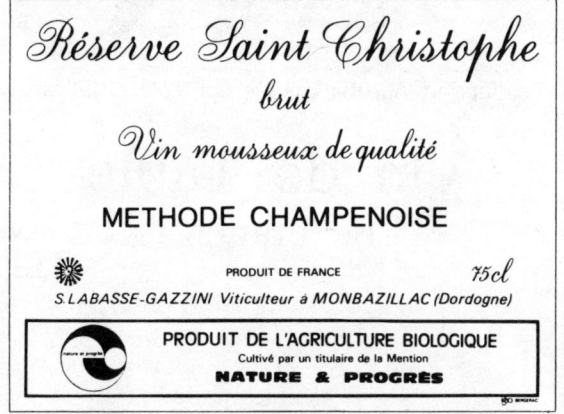

RÉSERVE ST. CHRISTOPHE. METHODE CHAMPENOISE. w.
Nature et Progrès.

THE ORGANIC WINE GUIDE

Jacques-Victor Mornai (M et Mme Labasse-Gazzini), Chateau le Barradis, 24240 Sigoules, Monbazillac, DORDOGNE. tel 53 58 30 01

NV w Light and refreshing, there were good bubbles, fruit and acidity. 'Not to be taken too seriously', joked one taster.

Méthode Champenoise. This wine had a good mousse and a slightly yeasty, fruity nose, similar to the flavour. Well liked by everyone who thought it a good champagne substitute.

FRANCE – RHONE VALLEY

TERRES BLANCHES. AC CÔTEAUX D'AIX EN PROVENCE LES BAUX. w.r.rosé
Terre et Vie. 190,000 bottles p.a. 50 Hl/hectare
Noël Michelin, Terres Blanches, 13210 Saint-Remy-de-Provence, AIX EN PROVENCE. tel 90 95 91 66

Noël Michelin has been making wine since 1973 and tries to preserve a natural equilibrium with the soil as well as creating a healthy wine. He grows a great number of wines but Grenache predominates in the reds, (although he did make a Cuvée Aurélia in 1985 with mostly Cabernet Sauvignon), Cabernet, Grenache and Cinsault for the rosé and 100% Ugni Blanc for the white.

'86 w People liked the "toasted manure" and "interesting rot" in the bouquet of this one, and although neutral in nature they liked the boiled sweets, strong flavour but expressed doubts about some bitterness in the aftertaste.

'84 r Some liked the high-toned, sweet metallic start but on the whole found the taste edgy, metallic and muddy.

VIN DE TABLE-JOUGLA. r
L.C. Jougla, La Pinarderie, 34370 Cazouls-les-Béziers, HÉRAULT

NV Bright, medium purply red, this wine had a nose of fruit rather than sweetness or jam, was balanced with good fruit and body, and was considered very drinkable.

THE RHONE VALLEY

The Rhône valley region stretches from Vienne in the north to just south of Avignon and although this falls between the same latitudes as Bordeaux the climate is much hotter and drier and generally speaking produces wines of a completely different character. The first vineyard in the area is said to have been planted by Phoenicians just outside Vienne over 2,000 years ago. The Romans certainly developed this and by the fourth century Hermitage and Côte Rôtie are being mentioned by name. In the 12th century the Knights Templar planted the vineyards that produce Châteauneuf-du-Pape and these were extended by Pope Jean XXII two centuries later. Over the last few years there has been a lot of promotional work done for the region and there are now several Routes des Vins, with signposts painted by Georges Mathieu, which involve scenic routes of the area with convenient pit stops to sample the local products; there is also a Université du Vin which runs courses for amateurs and professionals alike.

The region falls into four areas, the Côte Rôtie in the north, Hermitage and Die to the east, and the area Orange and Avignon which produces most of the general Côtes du Rhône as well as the well-known Châteauneuf-du-Pape.

As mentioned earlier, Hermitage has been producing wine for centuries and although considered to be undervalued a few years ago, it is now the region's most expensive wine, no longer a cheaper alternative to clarets and Burgundies. Although a wine in its own right, it is mentioned in Fielding's novels, a large proportion of the production was sold to Bordeaux to beef up some clarets, and indeed it is such a large wine it needs at least 10 to 20 years in bottle.

The wine from the Côte Rôtie, literally the roasted hillside, has more finesse than some other Rhône wines because of its northern position, but it can in no way be considered a light wine; made from the Syrah grape, it is considered necessary to blend in a quantity of juice from the white Viognier grape to lighten up the very dark tannic base. The white wine made from the Viognier grape called Condrieu, a unique wine which is very inadequately described as floral and spicy.

Similar in style but less weighty is the wine grown around Hermitage called Crozes-Hermitage and just to the south is another dark tannic wine that needs keeping called Cornas which is quickly gaining in popularity and price.

Off to the east of the Rhône is the area Clairette de Die which may have vineyards dating back to the first century AD. Most of the wine here is made into slightly sweet sparklers; traditionally this is done by allowing the wine to finish fermentation in the bottle but more commonly by méthode champenoise.

FRANCE – RHONE VALLEY

The southern Côtes du Rhône comprises several areas, such as Côteaux du Tricastin, Côtes du Ventoux, Côtes du Vivarais, Lirac, Luberon and Tavel. Apart from the general appellation Côtes du Rhônes and the wines from certain areas there are Côtes du Rhône Villages which are generally more refined and can become appellations in their own right, e.g. Gigondas. The most famous wine of the region is Châteauneuf-du-Pape, a wine unique in that it can be made from up to 13 different grape varieties. Grenache is the main grape with Cinsault, Syrah, Mourvèdre and even some whites going into the slow-maturing blend. The Perrin family who make Chateau de Beaucastel, one of the more renowned Châteauneuf-du-Papes has developed a way of dispensing with sulphur dioxide altogether. A brother, Jean-Pierre Perrin, makes a Côtes du Ventoux, Côtes du Rhône and a Beaumes de Venise using the trade name La Vieille Ferme.

Vincent Achard who makes Clairette de Die

THE ORGANIC WINE GUIDE

Château de Beaucastel. AC Châteauneuf-du-Pape. r
228,000 bottles p.a. 25 Hl/hectare
Ste. Ferme des Vignobles Perrin, Château de Beaucastel, 84350 Courthezon, VAUCLUSE. tel 90 70 70 60

The Perrin family have been making wine for four generations and both use traditional methods such as large stone vats for long fermentation and new techniques such as inert gas to prevent infection or oxidation; for example, they have done away with the use of sulphur dioxide. Using all 13 of the permitted grape varieties they mature the wine for two years in oak and the result is a very big flavoursome wine that will last for 10 to 20 years.

'82 Surprisingly light in colour with tons of fruit and tannin, we all knew we should have kept this for a long time, which is not to say it was not a pleasure to taste. This showed real class.

Châteauneuf-du-Pape. AC. r
P. André, Courthezon, VAUCLUSE

'82 Reticent at first, there was a peppery deep nose and in the mouth it was obviously well made with good fruit and length; it had finesse.

Clairette de Die. AC Clairette de Die. w
Nature et Progrès. 65,000 bottles p.a. 60 Hl/hectare
GAEC Achard-Vincent, Ste. Croix, 26150 Die, DIE. tel 75 22 11 22

Monsieur Achard has been adhering to the Nature et Progrès method since 1983 but he and his father before him have been making wine since 1860. They make this sparkling wine in two ways on the estate. Our favourite is the traditional way; in October the must is fermented very slowly at five degrees C until January. The wine is then bottled and the residual grape sugar permits a second fermentation; this produces a delicate mousse and preserves the delicious muscat flavour. The other way they make this wine is by the méthode champenois where they also use Muscat as well as Clairette grapes.

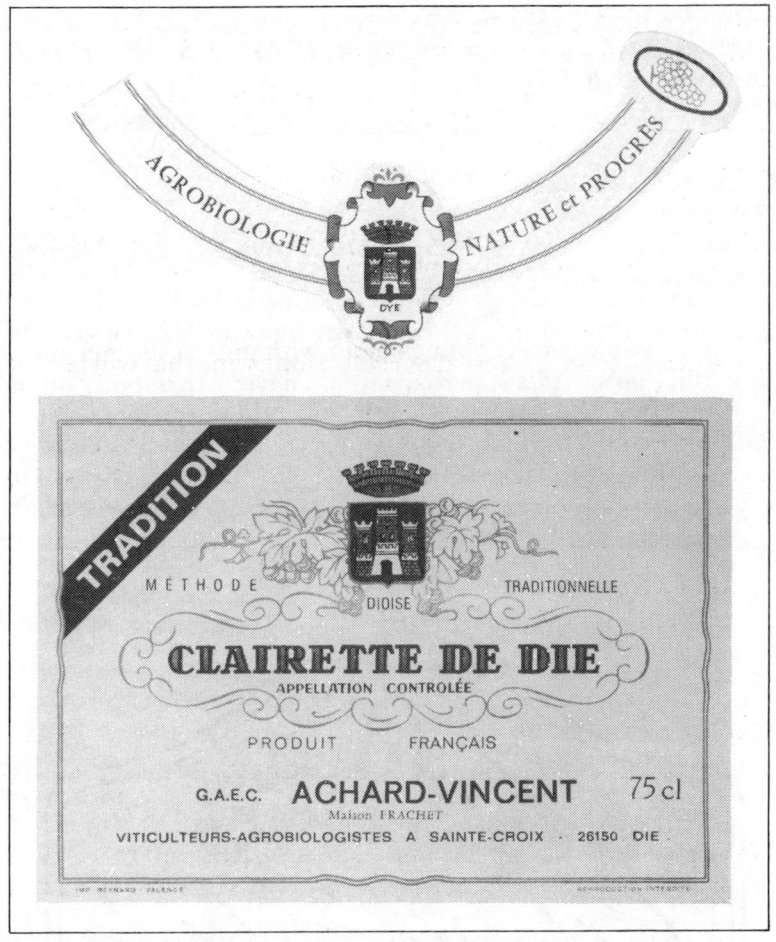

Tradition NV With a pleasantly clean colour and a lovely yeasty and muscaty nose, this slightly sweet but very fruity, strong and perfumed wine would be ideal with strawberries and cream. An interesting note – this bottle left, half drunk and uncorked for 18 hours still had masses of fizz.

Méthode Champenoise. NV. More clairette than muscat this had a distinct yeasty nose and a full, fry, fruity flavour with a honeyed background, and a good finish.

THE ORGANIC WINE GUIDE

CÔTEAUX DU TRICASTIN. AC. r.w
Jacques Jalifier, Baume de Transit, 26130 St. Paul Trois Châteaux, DROME

CÔTES DU RHÔNE. AC. r
Nature et Progrès
Cave Co-op. Comtadine-Dauphinoise, Puymeras, 84110 Vaison la Romaine, VAUCLUSE. tel 90 46 40 78

'85 This had a typically young colour with pink at the rim and a ripe fruity nose. It had, perhaps, more flavour than body but it had good acidity, reasonable length and a slight spiciness on the finish.

FRANCE – RHONE VALLEY

CÔTES DU RHÔNE. AC. r
Nature et Progrès. 10,000 bottles p.a. 40-50 Hl/hectare
Cave *"La Vigneronne", 84110 Villedieu, VAUCLUSE. tel 90 36 23 11*

With a co-operative decision following increasing consumer demand the people at "La Vigneronne" decided to farm organically and to use Nature et Progrès two years ago. They use the traditional grapes Grenache, Cinsault, Syrah and Mourvèdre.

'85 With fresh clean Rhône fruit and a slight spiciness on the nose, this turned out to be typical, rich and good with a surprisingly generous burst of fruit. The only quibble was with its length.

'86 Giving pink hints in the colour, the light, bright citrus flavours belied the 14% alcohol. There was not a lot of tannin and it came across as a well-made, attractive, drinkable wine.

THE ORGANIC WINE GUIDE

CÔTES DU RHÔNE. AC. r
Nature et Progrès
Daniel Combe, Vignoble de la Jasse, 84150 Violes, VAUCLUSE. tel 90 70 93 47

CÔTES DU RHÔNE. AC. r
Nature et Progrès. 27,000 bottles p.a.
Co-op. Vinicole de Nyonsais, Place Olivier de Serres, 26110 Nyons, DROME. tel 75 26 03 44

CÔTES DU RHÔNE. AC. r
Nature et Progrès. 4,000 bottles p.a.
Michel Delacroix, Avenue de la Gare, 30390 Théziers, GARD. tel 66 57 57 18

This family business has been growing organically since 1972 and also makes red, white and rosé vin de table.

CÔTES DU RHÔNE. AC. r
Nature et Progrès
Marcel Millet, Quartier St. Blaise, 84500 Bollène, VAUCLUSE. tel 90 30 46 07

CÔTES DU RHÔNE VILLAGE. AC. r
Paulette Pouizin, Quartier du Gibard, 84600 Visan, VAUCLUSE

CROZES-HERMITAGE. AC. r.w
Lemaire-Boucher. 15,000 bottles p.a. 35 Hl/hectare
Madame A. Begot, "Le Village", Serves sur Rhône, 26600 Tain l'Hermitage, DROME. tel 75 03 30 27

Safeguarding nature and the health of the consumer are the reasons the Begots have been making organic wine for the past 20 years. Syrah is the only grape used for the red and Marsanne (a northern Rhône grape that can smell a bit like glue) for the white.

'83 r A light but complex nose, disappointed on the palate, causing some people to comment "tight and tart" and "thin" but others found it "sound and typical".

FRANCE – RHONE VALLEY

DOMAINE DU BOIS NOIR. AC CÔTES DU RHÔNE. r.w.rosé
Jean-Pierre Estève, Domaine du Bois Noir, 27790 Baume de Transit, DROME. tel 75 98 11 02

DOMAINE LES CARDELINES. AC CÔTES DU RHÔNE. r
Nature et Progrès
Jean-Pierre Guintrand, La Thèzane, 84190 Vacqueyras, VAUCLUSE

DOMAINE DES CÈDRES. AC CÔTES DU RHÔNE. r.w.rosé
FNAB. 55,000 bottles p.a.
Dominique Pons, Domaine des Cèdres, St. Nazaire, 30200 Bagnols-sur-Cèze, GARD. tel 66 89 99 31

Comprising 30 acres, these vineyards have been worked organically for the past 15 years and half the production is sold in West Germany and Holland.

THE ORGANIC WINE GUIDE

DOMAINE DES COCCINELLES. AC CÔTES DU RHÔNE. r
Nature et Progrès
René Fabre, Domaine des Coccinelles, 30390 Domazan, GARD. tel 66 57 03 07

This estate of 15 hectares is named after the ladybird, eater of aphids and other undesirable insects.

'85 Purply pink in colour, this was a light and dry wine with some spice in the flavour; reminding one taster of a blended Beaujolais, it was generally well liked but one or two had reservations about its body.

René Fabre and Judy Kendrick, organic wine importer

FRANCE – RHONE VALLEY

DOMAINE RICHAUD. AC CÔTES DU RHÔNE AND CÔTES DU RHÔNE VILLAGE. r
Domaine Marcel Richaud, Route de Rasteau, 84290 Cairanne, VAUCLUSE. tel 90 30 85 25

This vineyard of 50 acres looks down on the village of Cairanne which gained the appellation Côtes du Rhône Village in 1967 along with only 16 other villages as a reward for their constant efforts to maintain quality. The wines are made from Grenache, Syrah and Carignan with a touch of Mourvèdre in the Côtes du Rhône. 95% of their exports end up in Holland.

DOMAINE SAINT-APOLLINAIRE. AC CÔTES DU RHÔNE. r.w
Biodynamique. 10,000 bottles p.a. 30-40 Hl/hectare
Daumas SCA, Domaine St-Apollinaire, Puymeras, 84110 Vaison-la-Romaine, VAUCLUSE

Monsieur Daumas has been making wine on this domaine since 1974 and grows Syrah, Grenache, Cinsault, Mourvèdre, Clairette, Ugni Blanc and Viognier from which he makes a variety of wines such as a Cêpage Viognier, a Blanc de Blanc, a Cuvée d'Apolline and a Cêpage Syrah.

'83 r We were all looking forward to this Côte du Rhône but we were sadly disappointed. "Medicinal" and "effluent from a Michelin tyre factory" described this wine; another thought a chemist in a lab could have done better.

DYNORGA. VIN DE TABLE. r.rosé
Biodynamie
Daumas SCA, Domaine St-Apollinaire, Puymeras, 84110 Vaison-la-Romaine, VAUCLUSE

NV. r This wine had a sickly appearance and reminded us all of cough bottles and disinfectant; those brave enough to taste it found pepper and sawdust.

MUSCAT DE BEAUMES DE VENISE-LA VIEILLE FERME. AC. w
M. Perrin, La Vieille Ferme, Route de Jonquières, Orange, VAUCLUSE

In France they drink this wine as an apéritif and with some cheeses but to our mind it is a dessert wine which is great with fruit.

NV Lovely golden hues, reminding one taster of polished brass, prefaced a delicate, spicy, tea-like nose. It had a well-defined, generous flavour and was sophisticated and obviously rich without being cloying.

LA VIEILLE FERME. AC CÔTES DE VENTOUX. r
M. Perrin, La Vieille Ferme, Route de Jonquières, Orange, VAUCLUSE

'85 With a good, deep colour and a nose that reminded somebody of shoe shops, this was a bit of a disappointment. Possibly suffering from bottle sickness, it was unpleasantly farmyardy, tasted of cardboard and made one think of headaches. He also makes a Côtes du Rhône under the same name.

FRANCE – RHONE VALLEY

VIGNOBLES DE LA JASSE. AC CÔTES DU RHÔNE. r
Nature et Progrès
Daniel Combe, Vignobles de la Jasse, 84150 Violes, VAUCLUSE. tel 90 70 93 47

'85 A full bouquet with an attractive hint of dirt and fully integrated flavour and tannin made one taster declare this wine "excellent". Light, fruity and balanced, this is one of the wines people went back to and drank after a tasting.

OTHER FRENCH ORGANIC WINE PRODUCERS

BONDAGON. VIN DE TABLE. w

NV Pale gold in colour, this had a fresh grapy nose and a flavour of tart Sauvignon and a touch of something more exotic. It was considered characterful quaffing although there was a sharp aftertaste.

CLAIRBIO

This méthode champenoise is made from Ugni Blanc and Clairette.

NV w This had no obvious faults but lacked any real interest or oomph.

LE CLOS DES GRIVES. AC CÔTES DU JURA. r.w
Nature et Progrès
Claude Charbonnier, Le Clos des Grives, Chille, 39000 Lons, JURA

He also makes a sparkler and vins de table.

CLOS PETRA ROSSA. AC CORSE. r.rosé
Nature et Progrès
François Franscisci, Clos Petra Rossa, Rue du Gal Graziani, 20220 l'Île Rousse, CORSE. tel 96 60 11 85

CLOS ST. MARTIN. VINS DE TABLE
Nature et Progrès
Augustin Coronat, Clos St. Martin, 20 Chemin Lamartine, 66430 Bompas. tel 68 63 26 09

CÔTEAUX D'AJACCIO. AC. r.w.
GAEC Martini-Ledentu, Lupena, 20000 Ocana-Cauro, CORSE

CÔTES DE TOUL. VINS DE TABLE. r.w
Nature et Progrès
Michel Goujot, 57 Chef Rue, Lucey, 4200 Toul. tel 83 43 82 26

CUVÉE DE LA BOISSIÈRE. VIN CHAMPAGNISÉ. w
Nature et Progrès
Jacques et Dany Blanchard, Boutièrs, 16100 Cognac, CHARENTE. tel 45 32 19 58

DOMAINE MARTINI. AC CÔTEAUX D'AJACCIO
Nature et Progrès
GAEC de Biso, Domaine Martini, Eccica Suarella, 20117 Cauro, CORSE. tel 93 46 88 71

MAS DES GARRIGUES. VINS DE TABLE
Nature et Progrès
Robert Planiol, Mas des Garrigues, Lecques, 30250 Sommières. tel 66 80 13 08

PINEAU DES CHARENTES. w.rosé
Nature et Progrès
Jacques et Dany Blanchard, Boutièrs, 16100 Cognac, CHARENTE. tel 45 32 19 58

Not strictly speaking a wine at all, being made from grape juice and brandy; used as an apéritif in France.

FRANCE – RHONE VALLEY

PINEAU DES CHARENTES
Lemaire-Boucher
Georges et Guy Pinard, GAEC de la Tour Verte, 16200 Foussignac, CHARENTE. tel 45 81 14 55

They also make Cognac, a sparkler and a dry white.

ST CHRISTOPHE. w
Méthode Champenoise.

GERMANY

German wines are a bit of a paradox in Britain today. The large sales of Liebfraumilch and such suggest a popularity with the public (and certainly the trade is largely supported by such sales) yet with the slightly more discerning wine drinker it is probably only second to South Africa in unpopularity (for different reasons of course). The champions enthuse about the unique balance between fruit and acidity, and the transforming powers of age, while the denigrators speak of a tart, insipid drink that is distinctly untrustworthy and unpleasant.

While there is certainly a trend amongst German winemakers to concentrate on making very dry (trocken) wines, would be foolish to believe the generalisations that are bandied about; as in most things vinous we would suggest you keep an open mind and trust your palate.

Wine artefacts in Germany date back to the sixth century BC and are of Greek origin as was, probably, the wine that was drunk from them. It is generally considered that the wine vine was imported with the Roman legions, or the people supplying them, and written sources suggest that vineyards were established on the banks of the Rhine and Moselle by the second or third century AD.

After the retreat of the Romans Charlemagne and the Franks developed the interest in viticulture by legislating about the training and treatment of vines and giving land that included vineyards as political gifts; wine was also seen in terms of the social graces. The Church developed the vineyards and viticulture during the Dark Ages and although the original

GERMANY

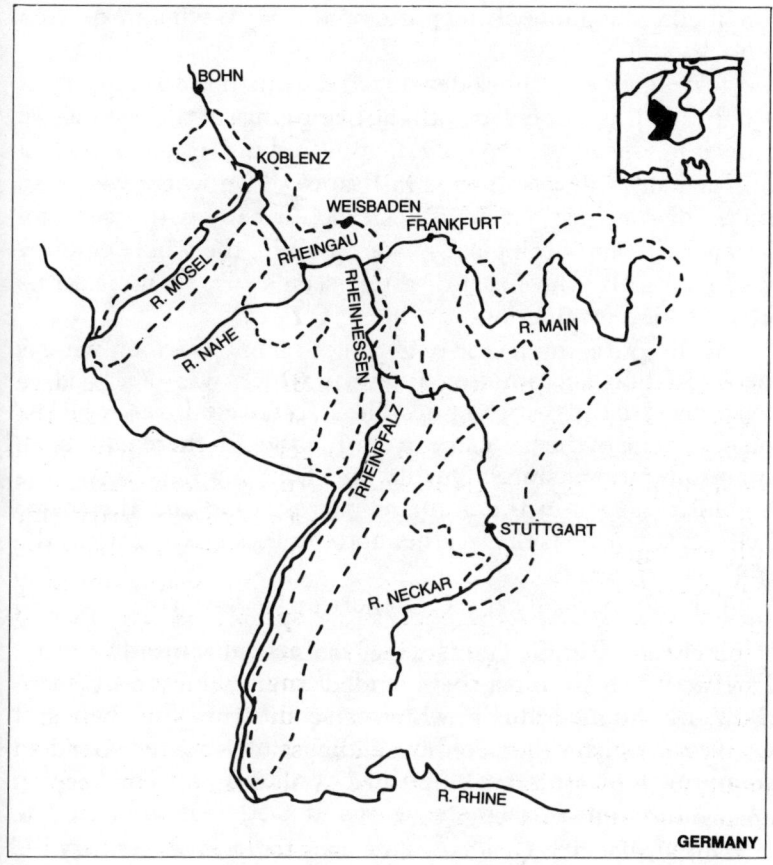

vineyards were low-lying, on the banks of the Rhine and Moselle, patches of forest were cleared on south-facing slopes and other advantaged sites and the vines moved up on to the hillsides.

The bulk of the trade that developed was to Northern Europe, and after Britain's loss of Bordeaux in 1453 and the consequent increase in price of French wine, Britain too began importing "Rhenish" and it was well established as a popular drink by the time of Cromwell and Charles II. Incidentally, "hock" as a name for German wine comes from the word Hockamore which is an anglicised version of Hochheimer,

Hochheim being one of the ports on the Main which exported wine.

A taste for vintage hock developed during the 18th century in Britain and this coincided with the beginnings of the trade as we know it in Germany. *Phylloxera* appeared in Germany in 1875 but was not as devastating as in France. Two world wars also caused disruption; but now Western Germany with its strong Green Party and ecologically aware public, the whole country was shocked by the Basel disaster, seems sure to increase its organic wine production.

One discouraging factor in getting to know German wine is the legislation surrounding it. That which was designed to make clear, to the British mind at least, often confuses. The last major change in the law came in 1971, although there have been minor alterations since. Quality and labelling depend on the amount of sugar in the grape at harvest time and the major factor in this level is the weather and to a lesser extent when the grape is harvested.

There are basically three categories:

1. Tafelwein. Simply "table wine"; this divides into Deutsche Tafelwein which must be blended from wines only from Germany and the ordinary which can come from anywhere and is given German character by adding unfermented German grape must (süssreserve). A third type is Landwein, which must come from a designated area and is equivalent to vins de pays; they are always dry.

2. Qualitätswein bestimmter Anbaugebeit or QbA. This is a "quality wine from a designated area" and this designated area can be a region, a subregion, a vineyard group or a single vineyard. They can also have sugar added to them.

3. Qualitätswein mit Prädikat or QmP. This is a "quality wine with special attributes" and must come from one of 11 designated regions. The original sugar content of the grape is specified by regulation, and in ascending order of sugar level will say on the label:

> Kabinett – normal harvest or what you would expect to find in the wine-maker's cupboard.

Spätlese – late-gathered grapes.
Auslese – late-gathered but selected grapes.
Beerenauslese – very ripe, late-gathered selected grapes.
Trockenbeerenauslese – noble rot grapes.
Eiswein – wine made from grapes left to freeze on the stalk; the water is frozen leaving only sweetness, fruit and acidity to make the wine.

These last three categories are always very expensive wines due to rarity value and labour costs.

Things are a bit complicated, however, by the variations in taste of the different regions and markets. In some areas people have a taste for sweeter wines and in others for drier, so the wine-makers adjust the sweetness or otherwise of the fermented wine by adding unfermented grape must or by fermenting the must to complete dryness. In the past cold cellars and sulphur dioxide would stop the fermentation thus leaving some residual sweetness in the wine.

The German organic certifications are Bioland, Naturland, Oinos, Biokreis and Demeter; most of these are affiliated to the Bundesverband Okologischer Weinbau (BOW).

BADEN

In the Middle Ages Baden was the largest wine producer and in spite of the ravages of the Thirty Years War was still the largest in 1800. However, after *phylloxera* and two world wars the area was viticulturally in bad shape, but since 1950 an enormous effort has been made; entire vineyards have been dug up, pushed into more advantageous slopes by earth-movers and replanted with new grape stocks. There are very few individual properties, most of the vineyards being worked by co-operatives, and it is now the third-largest producing area in Germany. Most of the production is white, with a little weissherbst (rosé) and the wine produced is amongst the most diverse in style in Germany.

THE ORGANIC WINE GUIDE

BAHLINGER SILVERBERG
Bioland/BOW. 20,000 litres p.a. 60 Hl/hectare
Weingut Rebschneckle Gerda Schmidd-Labudde und Klaus Labudde, Reidengartenstrasse 35, 7817 Ihringen am Kaisersthul. tel 07668 7213

Wines produced: Muller Thurgau QbA, Weissburgunder Kabinett, Spätburgunder Weissherbst (rosé) Kabinett.

Gerda Schmidd-Labudde and Klaus Labudde have been making organic wine for six years and started doing so to spare the environment and to reduce the use of chemical fertilisers; they cite the Sandoz incident at Basel which poisoned the Rhine. All the wines they produce are dry.

Muller Thurgau '86 This had a pleasantly flowery nose and a well-balanced sparkly lemon taste with a touch of pepper.

BAHLINGER SILVERBERG
BOW
Weingut Hans-Peter Trautwein, Bachstr. 19, 7836 Bahlingen. tel 07663 2650

GERMANY – BADEN

With a vineyard of 3.5 hectares Hans-Peter Trautwein started producing organic wine in 1980 as a protest against a nuclear power reactor in a neighbouring village and because he had had enough of chemical pesticides. Wines produced: Spätburgunder QbA, Muller Thurgau QbA, Weissburgunder QbA, Grauburgunder QbA.

Weissburgunder '86 This had a concentrated nose with a hint of wood but disappointed in the mouth; it was gravelly and hollow and somebody commented on "a bit of empty space".

Grauburgunder '86 This one split the company. Some thought it had an attractive soft nose with good fruit and acidity, whereas others found it austere, unbalanced and with a metallic finish.

Muller Thurgau Halbtrocken '86 From soft fruit through perfumed soap to diesel ran the initial comments on this one. On the palate it was very light and watery, had no length and someone commented on an unfortunate steely taste.

BALLRECHTER CASTELBERG
Biologisch-Ökologisch. 1-3,000 bottles p.a. 40 Hl/hectare
Weingut Kopfer, 7813 Staufen-Grunern. tel 07633 5288

Gerd Kopfer has been making organic wine for 10 years for ecological reasons. Wines produced: Nobling Spätlese.

'83 The Nobling grape is a cross between Silvaner and Gutedel (Chasselas), popular in Baden, which produces a must with a high sugar content such as this example. There was an attractive hint of rot on the nose and it was grapy, sweet, refreshing and mouth-filling. This is the sort of wine that might encourage the unenthusiastic to seek other German wines. Although considered drinkable and delicious it was probably too young.

BICKENSOHLER STEINFELSEN
Bioland/BOW. 20,000 litres p.a. 60 Hl/hectare
Weingut Rebschneckle, Gerda Schmid-Labudde und Klaus

THE ORGANIC WINE GUIDE

Labudde, Riedengartenstr. 35, 7817 Ihringen. tel 07668 7213
Wines produced: Gewurztraminer Spätlese Trocken.

BICKENSOHLER VULKANFELSEN
Bioland/BOW. 20,000 litres p.a. 60 Hl/hectare
Weingut Rebschneckle, Gerda Schmid-Labudde und Klaus Labudde, Riedengartenstr. 35, 7817 Ihringen. tel 07668 7213
Wines produced: Gewurztraminer Spätlese.

BURKHEIMER FEURBERG
Bioland/BOW. 20,000 litres p.a. 60 Hl/hectare
Weingut Rebschneckle, Gerda Schmid-Labudde und Klaus Labudde, Riedengartenstr. 35, 7817 Ihringen. tel 07668 7213

Wines produced: Weissburgunder QbA, Rulander QbA, Spätburgunder Weissherbst QbA.

GRUNERNER ALTENBERG
Biologisch-Ökologisch. 1-3,000 bottles p.a. 40 Hl/hectare
Weingut Kopfer, 7813 Staufen-Grunern. tel 07633 5288

GERMANY – BADEN

Wines produced: Muller Thurgau Kabinett Trocken, Muller Thurgau Trocken.

Muller Thurgau Kabinett Trocken '85 This had a good colour and was fresh, grapy and slightly spritzig in the mouth. It was maybe a bit ordinary but would make a good apéritif.

Muller Thurgau Trocken '84 There was a slightly sticky nose of sweetness rather than fruit but in the mouth it was tart, tart, tart.

IHRINGER FOHRENBERG
Bioland/BOW. 20,000 litres p.a. 60 Hl/hectare
Weingut Rebschneckle, Gerda Schmid-Labudde und Klaus Labudde, Riedengartenstr. 35, 7817 Ihringen. tel 07668 7213

Wines produced: Silvaner QbA, Silvaner Spätlese, Gewurztraminer Kabinett.

LAUFENER ALTENBERG
Bioland/BOW. 20,000 litres p.a. 60 Hl/hectare
Weingut Rebschneckle, Gerda Schmid-Labudde und Klaus Labudde, Riedengartenstr. 35, 7817 Ihringen. tel 07668 7213

Wines produced: Gutedel QbA.

MERDINGER BUHL
Biologisch-Organischem. 8,300 litres p.a. 70 Hl/hectare
Weingut Sonnenwirbele, Anne Pefchlow, Kai Schuhmacher, Michael Doub, Bahnhofstrasse 7, Ihringen 7817. tel 07668 803

These people want no more poison in agriculture and to this end have been using organic methods to make wine for the past six years. Wines produced: Muller Thurgau QbA, Muller Thurgau Kabinett, Silvaner Spätlese, Weissburgunder Kabinett, Gewurztraminer Spätlese, Rulander QbA, Rulander Spätlese, Spätburgunder Weissherbst and Spätburgunder Rotwein.

Muller Thurgau Trocken '86 There was a nice spicy tartness about this one with a touch of sherbet, but like sherbet it faded fast.

Spätburgunder. Weissherbst (rosé) '86 "A sour nothing wine". It was flat.

MOSEL-SAAR-RUWER

This is a large region and although the wines from the three areas can be distinguished by the locals or by an experienced palate, they still have a commonality. Some of the production is pretty thin and weedy but some of the Rieslings are considered among the best in the world; Frank Schoonmaker, a writer on German wine, refers to them as having "a honeyed fragrance like a bunch of spring flowers". Few of them are made for ageing and the region is renowned (or infamous) for such well-known names as Piesporter Michelsberg, Bereich Bernkastel and Moselblümchen. It used to be virtually all Riesling that was grown but in part it has been replaced by the more reliable Muller Thurgau and the newer varieties such as Kerner. Even now some 40% of the vines are original pre-*phylloxera* European stock. It is the fourth-largest wine-producing region in Germany.

BRIEDELER HERZCHEN
Bioland/BOW. 18,000 bottles p.a. 100 Hl/hectare
*Weingut Harald Steffens, Hauptstr. 178, 5589 Briedel/Mosel.
tel 06542 41184*

The Riesling predominates in this vineyard on the steep slopes of the Mosel valley. The wines are bottled in the spring and contain a relatively high carbonation content and they are always dry with a low alcohol content. Herr Steffens started making wine in 1982 to help control pollution, improve wine quality and contribute to a healthier lifestyle. Wines made: Riesling Trocken QbA.

GERMANY – MOSEL-SAAR-RUWER

Riesling Trocken '86 This had a lemon nose although it was a bit weak and flowery; it was dry and tart and cleaned rather than filled the mouth, but overall it was not too bad.

BRIEDELER NONNENGARTEN
Bioland/BOW. 18,000 bottles p.a. 100 Hl/hectare
Weingut Harald Steffens, Hauptstr. 178, 5589 Briedel/Mosel. tel 06542 41184

Wines made: Riesling Kabinett Trocken

Riesling Kabinett Trocken '86 With a sharp, green apple nose, this had an oily, strong taste but was very tart and "makes your eyebrows rise". Two tasters found an unpleasant aftertaste.

KROVER PARADIES
Oinos. 3,000 bottles p.a. not known
Udo Wick, Stablostr. 37, 5563 Krov/Mosel. tel 06541 9674

Udo Wick has been producing organic wine since 1981 because he was not satisfied with conventional viticultural methods and because he wanted to start working against the pollution of the environment using his profession and in his area. It is unlikely that you will find any of his wine in Britain.

LANDWEIN DER MOSEL
Oinos/BOW. not known. 100 Hl/hectare
Weingut Frank Brohl, Bergstr. 7, 5586 Reil/Mosel. tel 06542 2954

Frank Brohl considers organic agriculture the best way by reason of logic and of taste. He is proud of what he does and thinks the consumer can be a bit proud about what he or she buys. Most of his vineyards are very steep so he cannot use machinery but he considers working by hand the most efficient way of controlling his work according to the Oinos standards. Landwein is the German equivalent to vins de pays and legally has to be half a degree stronger than tafelwein though dry.

THE ORGANIC WINE GUIDE

PUNDERICHER MARIENBURG
Oinos/BOW. not known. 100 Hl/hectare
Weingut Frank Brohl, Bergstr. 7, 5586 Reil/Mosel. tel 06542 2954

Wines produced: Riesling Kabinett Trocken

Riesling Kabinett '86 This had a rich Riesling nose and had some sparkle in the mouth but lacked fruit and died quickly.

REILER GOLDLAY
Oinos/BOW. not known. 100 Hl/hectare
Weingut Frank Brohl, Bergstr. 7, 5586 Reil/Mosel. tel 06542 2954

Wines produced: Riesling Kabinett

REILER MULLAY-HOFBERG
Oinos/BOW. not known. 100 Hl/hectare
Weingut Frank Brohl, Bergstr. 7, 5586 Reil/Mosel. tel 06542 2954

Wines produced: Riesling QbA, Kerner QbA

Riesling Trocken QbA '86 With an open Riesling nose, this had a refreshing acidity and some fruit to balance it; it was not as desperately dry as some.

Kerner QbA '86 Almost colourless, this had a distinct nose but was far too tart and fruitless for our taste.

REILER VOM HEISSEN STEIN
Oinos/BOW. not known. 100 Hl/hectare
Weingut Frank Brohl, Bergstr. 7, 5586 Reil/Mosel. tel 06542 2954

Wines produced: Kerner Spätlese Trocken

TRARBACHER SCHLOSSBERG
Bioland/BOW. 18,000 bottles p.a. 100 Hl/hectare
Weingut Harald Steffens, Hauptstr. 178, 5589 Briedel/Mosel. tel 06542 41184

Wines produced: Riesling Trocken QbA

GERMANY – THE NAHE

Riesling Trocken '86 Very pale in colour and with a gentle flowery nose this, unfortunately, had pungent fruit and a rasping finish.

Riesling Trocken '85 This had a cooked fruit nose and was simple and sharp in the mouth with a greengage acidity; "hard work" thought one taster.

THE NAHE

At the intersection of the Nahe and Rhine rivers the district produces a large variety of wines considering its size. Silvaner is the basic grape with lots of Muller Thurgau, and Riesling is regaining its popularity as a producer of quality. Not much of the area's production is exported.

GULDENTALER APOSTLEBERG
Bioland. 1-5,000 litres p.a. 70 Hl/hectare
Weingut Konrad Knodel, Kreuznacherstr. 23, 6531 Windesheim. tel 06707 232.

Wines produced: Müller Thurgau QbA.

Müller Thurgau QbAQ '86 Medium dry in style, this was soft and supple although one taster thought it hollow.

GULDENTALER SCHLOSSEKAPELLE
Bioland. 1-5,000 litres p.a. 70 Hl/hectare.
Weingut Konrad Knodel, Kreuznacherstr. 23, 6531 Windesheim. tel 06707 232.

WINDESHEIMER ROSENBERG
Bioland. 1-5,000 litres p.a. 70 Hl/hectare
Weingut Konrad Knodel, Kreuznacherstr. 23, 6531 Windesheim. tel 06707 232.

Wines produced: Scheurebe Kabinett, Kerner Spätlese, Riesling Spätlese, Gewurztraminer Auslese.

Riesling Spätlese '85 An attractive nose but dry and rasping in the mouth.

Gewurztraminer Auslese '83 A 'passable' nose but unfortunately no life or length.

RHEINHESSEN

The second-biggest producer of wine, this region is responsible for the likes of Liebfraumilch and Niersteiner. Liebfraumilch has a history stretching back centuries and was originally known as Liebfrauenmilch and referred to the wine made from the produce of the vineyards around the church Liebfrauenkirche in Worms. "Holy Lady's Milk" it may have been, but as its popularity spread so did the vineyards producing it. During the legislation of 1971 wine from the Nahe, Rheingau, Rheinhessen and Rheinpfaltz was permitted to use the name. However, some more legislation in 1982 reduced this to wine produced in Rheinhessen and Rheinpfalz. Reassuring, I think you will agree. Nierstein itself produces some fine wines but the name can be used for Niersteiner Gutes Domtal, a subregion comprising 15 villages or a larger area (Bereich) equal to a third of all Rheinhessen; surely this is an argument in itself for listing the smaller, more caring producers in this book. The area is mostly planted with Muller Thurgau but the best wine is still made from Riesling.

DEINHEIMER PATERHOF
BOW. 3-15,000 bottles p.a. 60 Hl/hectare
Weingut Brüder Dr. Becker, 6501 Ludwigshoe bei Oppenheim am Rhein. tel 06249 8430

Dating back to the 18th century, this vineyard developed from a small farm and is worked by the family with the help of two employees. They are involved in the peace movement and use organic methods to avoid polluting the environment and for

GERMANY – RHEINHESSEN

RHEINHESSEN
QUALITÄTSWEIN MIT PRÄDIKAT

1983
Riesling

DIENHEIMER PATERHOF SPÄTLESE

WEINGUT BRÜDER DR. BECKER LUDWIGSHÖHE
ERZEUGER-ABFÜLLUNG   AP NR. 4 371 018 12 85   0,75 L
MITGLIED IM VERBAND DEUTSCHER PRÄDIKATSWEINGÜTER E. V.

Christian reasons. 35% of the vineyard is planted with Riesling and the rest with Silvaner, Scheurebe, Muller Thurgau and Kerner. Wines made: Riesling Halbtrocken, Reisling Spätlese.

Riesling Halbtrocken '86 This had a sherbety lemon nose and was good, crisp and balanced; it was not at all austere but maybe a bit nervy and would make great summer drinking.

Riesling Spätlese '83 After an initial whiff of sulphur there was a lovely oily lanolin nose and a full-flavoured spicy ripeness developed in the glass; there was a short but lovely finish.

DEINHEIMER PATERHOF
BOW. 35,000 bottles p.a. 85 Hl/hectare
Weingut Franz-Joseph Duttenhofer, Kirchstr. 18, 6501 Deinheim. tel 06133 1366 oder 3443

Franz-Joseph Duttenhofer started experimenting with organic cultivation in 1977, expanded production, and since 1985 he has produced exclusively organic wines. "I started organic production in order to conserve nature and the environment, to

THE ORGANIC WINE GUIDE

protect the animals and organisms in the soils of the vineyards and last but not least for the health of the people who enjoy wine as a natural and pure product. The vines are fertilised with organic manure from horses and chickens, mineral additives and different sorts of plants growing between the vines and then ploughed under. Protection against fungal disease and pest control is done by useful insects and plant extracts. The use of fungicides, insecticides and acaricides is completely avoided." Wines produced: Kerner Kabinett, Rulander Spätlese, Rulander and Silvaner Spätlese Trocken, Silvaner and Silvaner Spätlese.

Kerner Kabinett '84 This had a slightly musty nose but had good width and body with a taste of grape seed. It had an abrupt finish.

Rulander Spätlese '84 A greeny, oily, rich nose was followed by an immediately attractive flavour that was complex without being heavy and had some length; it would be good with food.

Silvaner '84 This had a touch of pale colour and reminded tasters of corn-on-the-cob, buttered popcorn and rosewater. In

GERMANY – RHEINHESSEN

the mouth it was considered to be harmonious, mellow, oily and developed with good width.

Rulander and Silvaner Spätlese Trocken '85 Very pale in colour, this was delicately perfumed and had some lift and charm; it had good texture and weight but should have been richer with such a nose.

Silvaner Spätlese '83 With an elderflower nose, this wine had reasonable fruit but needs time to pick up the required oily characteristic; it had a refreshing finish.

DEINHEIMER TAFELSTEIN
BOW. 3-15,000 bottles p.a. 60 Hl/hectare
Weingut Brüder Dr. Becker, 6501 Ludwigshoe bei Oppenheim am Rhein. tel 06249 8430

Wines produced: Riesling Kabinett, Silvaner Kabinett

DEINHEIMER TAFELSTEIN
BOW. 35,000 bottles p.a. 85 Hl/hectare
Weingut Franz-Joseph Duttenhofer, Kirchstr. 18, 6501 Deinheim. tel 06133 1366 oder 3443

Silvaner Trocken '86 This wine was almost colourless and smelled like a flowery syrup; it was dry, flat and astringent and had no length.

THE ORGANIC WINE GUIDE

ENSHEIMER KOCHELBERG
Weingut Walter Hauck, 6509 Bermersheim, Rheinhessen. tel 06731 1272.

Wines produced: Riesling Kabinett

Riesling Kabinett '83 Showing some colour, this wine had an attractive nose, was balanced and developed well in the mouth.

FLONHEIMER PFAFFENBURG
Gebr Werner

'83 Pale yellow in colour, this had a nose of green grass and flowers although one person though it a bit smelly. It was round, oily and had good length, and overall was considered very pleasant.

GUNTERSBLUMER BORNPFAD
Bioland. 40,000 litres p.a. 57 Hl/hectare
Weingut Dr. Heinrich Schnell, 6524 Guntersblum am Rhein. tel 06249 2320

Burkhard Schnell began organic production in 1970 as a result of noticing that the number of butterflies was decreasing, so he

GERMANY – RHEINHESSEN

stopped using herbicides (to save their food) and insecticides (to save them). Wines produced: Muller Thurgau Kabinett.

GUNTERSBLUMER EISERNE HAND
Bioland. 40,000 litres p.a. 57 Hl/hectare
Weingut Dr. Heinrich Schnell, 6524 Guntersblum am Rhein. tel 06249 2320

Wines produced: Muller Thurgau Kabinett

GUNTERSBLUMER HIMMELTAL
Bioland. 40,000 litres p.a. 57 Hl/hectare
Weingut Dr. Heinrich Schnell, 6524 Guntersblum am Rhein. tel 06249 2320

Wines produced: Morio-Muskat Kabinett

GUNTERSBLUMER STEIG TERR
Bioland. 40,000 litres p.a. 57 Hl/hectare
Weingut Dr. Heinrich Schnell, 6524 Guntersblum am Rhein. tel 06249 2320

Wines produced: Traminer Spätlese, Silvaner Spätlese.

GUNTERSBLUMER VOGELSGARTEN
Bioland. 40,000 litres p.a. 57 Hl/hectare
Weingut Dr. Heinrich Schnell, 6524 Guntersblum am Rhein. tel 06249 2320

Wines produced: Silvaner QbA, Huxelrebe Kabinett, Scheurebe Kabinett.

Scheurebe Kabinett '86 This had the typical Scheurebe cat's piss nose, although not unattractive, and was green and prickly tart in the mouth and needed more fruit.

LONSHEIMER SCHONBERT
Gebr. Werner

Wines produced: Wurzer Auslese

The Wurzer is a cross between the Silvaner and Gewurztraminer.

THE ORGANIC WINE GUIDE

LUDWIGSHOHER TEUFELSKOPF
BOW. 3-15,000 bottles p.a. 60 Hl/hectare
Weingut Brüder Dr. Becker, 6501 Ludwigshoe bei Oppenheim am Rhein

Wines produced: Kerner Kabinett, Kerner Spätlese, Scheurebe Auslese, Silvaner

Silvaner '86 After a grapy, spicy nose the taste came as a bit of a disappointment. There was a touch of lemon and violets but it was basically flat and hollow with no development.

LUDWIGSHOHER TEUFELSKOPF
Bioland. 40,000 litres p.a. 57 Hl/hectare
Weingut Dr. Heinrich Schnell, 6524 Guntersblum am Rhein. tel 06249 2320

Wines made: Scheurebe Spätlese, Faberrebe Spätlese

METTENHEIMER
Naturland. 100,000 bottles p.a. 60 Hl/hectare
Weingut Sander, In den Weingarten, 6521 Mettenheim. tel 06242 1583

Wines produced: Kerner Kabinett, Fabberebe Kabinett, Reisling Kabinett

The Sanders have been making wine for 250 years but it was not until 30 years ago that Otto Heinrich Sander helped pioneer organic viticulture.

METTENHEIMER GOLDBERG
Naturland. 100,000 bottles p.a. 60 Hl/hectare
Weingut Sander, In den Weingarten, 6521 Mettenheim. tel 06242 1583

Wines made: Spätburgunder Weissherbst (rosé)

METTENHEIMER MICHELSBERG
Naturland. 100,000 bottles p.a. 60 Hl/hectare
Weingut Sander, In den Weingarten, 6521 Mettenheim. tel 06242 1583

Wines made: Riesling Kabinett

GERMANY – RHEINPFALZ

METTENHEIMER SCHLOSSBERG
Naturland. 100,000 bottles p.a. 60 Hl/hectare
Weingut Sander, In den Weingarten, 6521 Mettenheim. tel 06242 1583

Wines made: Riesling Spätlese

NIERSTEINER BRUDERSBERG
BOW. 150-200,000 litres p.a. 50-60 Hl/hectare
Weingut Freiherr Heyl zu Herrnsheim, Langgasse 3, D-6505 Nierstein. tel 06133 5120

This estate was bought by the great-grandfather of the present owner, the Baron Cornelius Heyl zu Herrnsheim, who was a Member of Parliament and initiator of the first German wine law in 1892. The estate not only cultivates parts of all the famous Nierstein vineyards but also experiments with new varietals in their own gardens. 59% of their planting is Riesling.

NIERSTEINER KRANZBERG
BOW. 150-200,000 litres p.a. 50-60 Hl/hectare
Weingut Freiherr Heyl zu Herrnsheim, Langgasse 3, D-6505 Nierstein. tel 06133 5120

Muller Thurgau Kabinett Trocken '85 The nose on this wine is characterless but in the mouth there was some personality and smoothness although one person thought it broom-like, "the flower if preferred".

Silvaner '82 Words used to describe this wine were earthy, awful, oily, metallic and, oddly, no taste.

RHEINPFALZ

This is the second-largest wine-making region in vineyard terms, but due to the fertility of the soil and the amount of sun it gets it produces the most wine. Known as the Palatinate in Britain, "pfalz" originally refers to the palaces built by the Roman Emperors on the Palatine Hill 2,000 years ago. Recently there has been a lot of investment in modern equipment and a lot of vineyards have been uprooted and rearranged with the help of earth-moving machines. Muller Thurgau is predominant and Portugieser is popular but Silvaner is on the way out. The wines tend to be fuller in body than those from the other regions, and they go much better with food.

Arzheimer Seligmacher
Bioland. 6-12,000 bottles p.a. 80-110 Hl/hectare
Wolfgang Marzolph, Schloss-Strasse 2B, 6740 Landau. tel 06341 84904

"After a nice time of life", working and travelling the world, Wolfgang Marzolph decided to follow in his great-grandfather's footsteps and produce wine for himself and live on it. He began using organic methods from the beginning and now has four hectares of land, half of which is vineyard and the rest orchard and wheatfield. His intention is to get away from the traditional monoculture of wine-growing and create a more ecologically sound system of survival.

Wines produced: Morio Muskat QbA, Muller Thurgau QbA, Muller Thurgau Spätlese, Spätburgunder Rotwein QbA, Silvaner Spätlese, Riesling Sekt.

Bochinger Rosenkranz
Bioland. 17,000 bottles p.a. Riesling 50 Hl/hectare. Muller Thurgau 90 Hl/hectare
Churpfalz-Keller Zellertal, 6719 Ottersheim, Obergasse 9. tel 06355 1285

They have been making organic wine here since 1980.

Wines made: Weissburgunder Kabinett.

Bochinger Rosenkranz
Bioland. 80 Hl/hectare
Weingut Gg. Messerschmitt, 6741 Bochingen, Burrweilerstr. 10. tel 06341 60854

GERMANY – RHEINPFALZ

Roswitha Schwarz has been using organic methods since 1980.

Wines produced: Heroldrebe Weissherbst Kabinett, Portugieser Rotwein Kabinett, Muller Thurgau Kabinett, Kerner Spätlese, Gewurztraminer Auslese.

DEIDESHEIMER HOFSTUCK
BOW. 15,000 litres p.a.
Weingut Rudolf Eymann, 6701 Gonnheim. tel 06322 2808

Rudolf Eymann and his team have been making organic wine for five years now because they believe it to be the only method with a real future.

Wines produced: Portugieser Trocken (red), Muller Thurgau Halbtrocken.

DIEDESFELDER REBSTOCKEL
Bioland. 60-80 Hl/hectare.
Weingut Fritz Breiling, 6735 Maikammer an der Weinstrasse, Bahnhofstr. 15, Rheinpfalz. tel 06321 5020.

The Breilings have been making wine since 1733 and have been using organic methods since 1965.

Wines produced: Portugeiser Spätlese.

DURKHEIMER FEURBERG
BOW. 15,000 litres p.a.
Weingut Rudolf Eymann, 6701 Gonnheim. tel 06322 2808

Wines produced: Riesling Trocken, Portugieser Trocken.

EDENKOBENER HEIDEGARTEN
Bioland. 60-80 Hl/hectare.
Weingut Fritz Breiling, 6753 Maikammer an der Weinstrasse, Bahnhofstr. 15, Rheinpfalz. tel 06321 5020.

Wines produced: Rulander Kabinett

THE ORGANIC WINE GUIDE

Rulander Kabinett '86 This had a richer nose than expected and reminded some of cider apples; it was full flavoured and had some development.

GONNHEIMER MANDELGARTEN
BOW. 15,000 litres p.a.
Weingut Rudolf Eymann, 6701 Gonnheim. tel 06322 2808

Wines produced: Gewurztraminer Trocken, Silvaner Trocken, Portugieser Trocken.

GONNHEIMER MARTINSHOHE
BOW. 15,000 litres p.a.
Weingut Rudolf Eymann, 6701 Gonnheim. tel 06322 2808

Wines produced: Gewurztraminer Beerenauslese, Rulander Auslese, Riesling Auslese

GONNHEIMER SONNENBERG
BOW. 15,000 litres p.a.
Weingut Rudolf Eymann, 6701 Gonnheim. tel 06322 2808

THE ORGANIC WINE GUIDE

Wines produced: Kerner Trocken, Spätburgunder Kabinett, Spätburgunder Spätlese.

MAIKAMMERER HEILIGENBERG
Bioland. 60-80 Hl/hectare.
Weingut Fritz Breiling, 6753 Maikammer an der Weinstrasse, Bahnhofstr. 15, Rheinpfalz. tel 06321 5020.

Wines produced: Morio Muskat Kabinett, Muller Thurgau Kabinett, Riesling Kabinett

MAIKAMMERER MANDELHOHE
Bioland. 60-80 Hl/hectare.
Weingut Fritz Breiling, 6753 Maikammer an der Weinstrasse, Bahnhofstr. 15, Rheinpfalz. tel 06321 5020.

Wines produced: Portugieser QbA, Kerner Kabinett, Spätburgunder Kabinett, Scheurebe Kabinett, Silvaner QbA

Portugieser QbA '86 A light, not unattractive colour and a fatty, toffee nose; it was stalky and had a light tannic aftertaste but had little character or taste.

Silvaner QbA '86 This had a typical Silvaner nose, was balanced and refreshing and not at all tart.

Neustädter Grain
Bioland. 17,000 bottles p.a. 50-90 Hl/hectare
Churpfalz-Keller Zellertal, 6719 Ottersheim, Obergasse 9. tel 06355 1285

Wines produced: Portugieser Trocken.

Pfalzer Landwein
Bioland. 60-80 Hl/Hectare.
Weingut Fritz Breiling, 6753 Maikammer an der Weinstrasse, Bahnhofstr. 15, Rheinpfalz. tel 06321 5020.

Wollemesheimer Mutterle
Bioland. 6-12,000 bottles p.a. 80-110, Hl/hectare
Wolfgang Marzolph, Schloss-Strasse 2B, 6740 Landau. tel 06341 84904

Wines produced: Spätburgunder Trocken, Muller Thurgau Spätlese, Silvaner Spätlese.

Zeller Kreuzberg
Bioland. 17,000 bottles p.a. 50-90 Hl/hectare
Churpfaltz-Keller Zellertal, 6719 Ottersheim, Obergasse 9. tel 06355 1285

Wines produced: Silvaner Kabinett.

ITALY

The history of wine certainly goes back at least 4,000 years to the times when the enterprising Phoenicians were colonising Sicily and Sardinia. The Greeks grew wine vines when they were in southern Italy and the Romans, of course, spread it through France, Germany and, to a lesser extent, Britain.

The reputation of Italian wine is changing from that of the cheap and cheerful to the more considered, almost designer expectations of the international market. A lot of wine merchants are certainly extending their Italian lists – while still selling a lot of Lambrusco.

The wine produced in Italy swings from the mass-exported container-loads of unfermented musts and cutting wine (nearly 50% of exports) to France, Germany and the USSR, to the £100 bottles of Brunello occasionally seen in specialist shops and Italian delicatessens. It is curious that France imports so much, but wines that are lacking in body can be marvellously improved when cut by another wine and those wines lacking in colour due to chemical overfertilisation can pick up some colour from a heavily pigmented Italian variety. Because of its northerly climate Germany does not produce enough bulk of its own so they too import lots of Italian must and wine to blend with their own to attain sufficient production.

Although a lot of Italians consider the laws against chaptalisation and chemical stabilising agents as an economic burden and are appealing against them to the EEC, they have been in the vanguard of cleaner wine production. While they do use sulphur dioxide at the pre-fermentation stage, they can only

THE ORGANIC WINE GUIDE

use a sixth of that permitted by the EEC and they avoid it completely at the pre-bottling stage. A lot of the whites, rosés and cheaper reds are flash-pasteurised (the temperature is quickly raised to kill bacteria), slow fermented, refrigerated and centrifuged (to clear the wine), filtered and then put into sterile bottles. The serious whites and reds are treated more

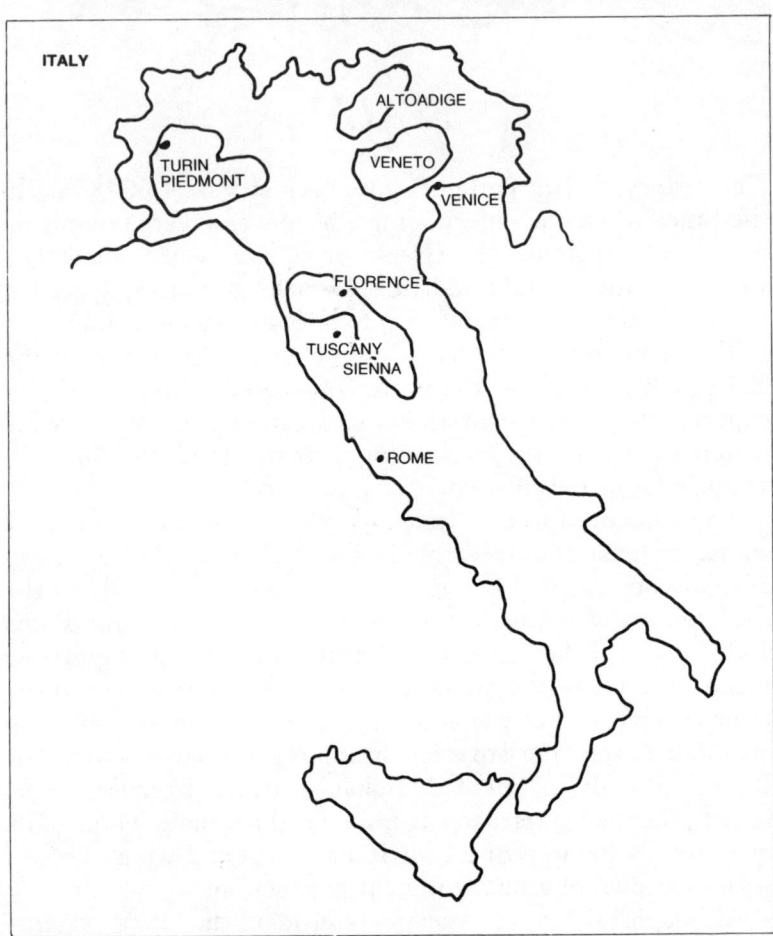

traditionally although there is a growing trend to mature in steel rather than wood in some vineyards.

The current wine legislation dates back to 1963 and is known

ITALY

as Denominazione di Origine Controllata (DOC) and the more recent Denominazione di Origine Controllata Garantita (DOCG) for the bigger-known names. This regulation specifies the colour, area or village, permitted grapes, minimum alcohol level and production and covers about 12% of the wine produced. Unfortunately these regulations severely limit the wine-maker and this results in a lot of interesting Italian wine being produced that is strictly speaking vino da tavola but commands more respect and money than a DOC. A more recent piece of regulation requires all Italian wine to get a highly priced health certificate before it can be exported. The Italian organic growers association is called the "Associazione Suolo e Salute" or the soil and health association, which is based in Turin.

BARDOLINO CHIARETTO. DOC. rosé
Azienda Agricola dei Conti Guerrieri-Rizzardi, Bardolino, 37011 Verona, VENETO

Antonio Rizzardi's family have owned this estate since the 18th century and have vineyards in Soave, Bardolino and Valpolicella.

NV Unlike a lot of rosés this was not like dentists' mouth-wash in appearance. It was dry and attractively balanced and had light, delicate, ripe fruit and was typically stalky with a good finish.

BIANCO TOSCANO-CASINA DI CORNIA. VINO DA TAVOLA. w
Nature et Progrès
Antoine Luginbuhl e Duccio Fontant, Casina di Cornia, 53011 Castellina in Chianti. tel 39/05 77 74 30 52

CHIANTI CLASSICO-CASINA DI CORNIA. DOC. r
Nature et Progrès
Antoine Luginbuhl e Duccio Fontant, Casina di Cornia, 53011 Castellina in Chianti. tel 39/05 77 74 30 52

THE ORGANIC WINE GUIDE

Chianti Putto-San Vito. DOC. r
Roberto Drighi

'85 With vanilla on the nose, this was strongly, flavoured with background fruit and an oaky flavour; there was a distinct tannic finish.

Gutturnio dei Colli Piacentini. r
Azienda Agricola Luzzano

This wine, made by the Fugazza sisters is mostly Barbera and

ITALY

comes from an up-and-coming area, the hilly area near Piacenza in the Apennine foothills.

'85 r Fruity on the nose and generously fruity in the mouth we thought this wine easy in a non-derogatory sense.

Poggio Alle Rocche. Vino da Tavola.
A. and L. Sircana, S and C. Pedicino. San Gimignano.

'85 This was pale lemon in colour and smelled of Cox's apples and white pepper; there was a pleasing astringency and sufficient body to make it good with chunky fish soup or spicy starters.

Rosso di Castellina. Vino da Tavola. r
Nature et Progrès
Antoine Luginbuhl e Duccio Fontant, Casina di Cornia, 53011 Castellina in Chianti. tel 39/05 77 74 30 52

ITALY

SOAVE CLASSICO. DOC. w
Azienda Agricola dei Conti Guerrieri-Rizzardi, Bardolino, 37011 Verona, VENETO

Made with 90% Garganega (the local Soave grape) and 10% Trebbiano.

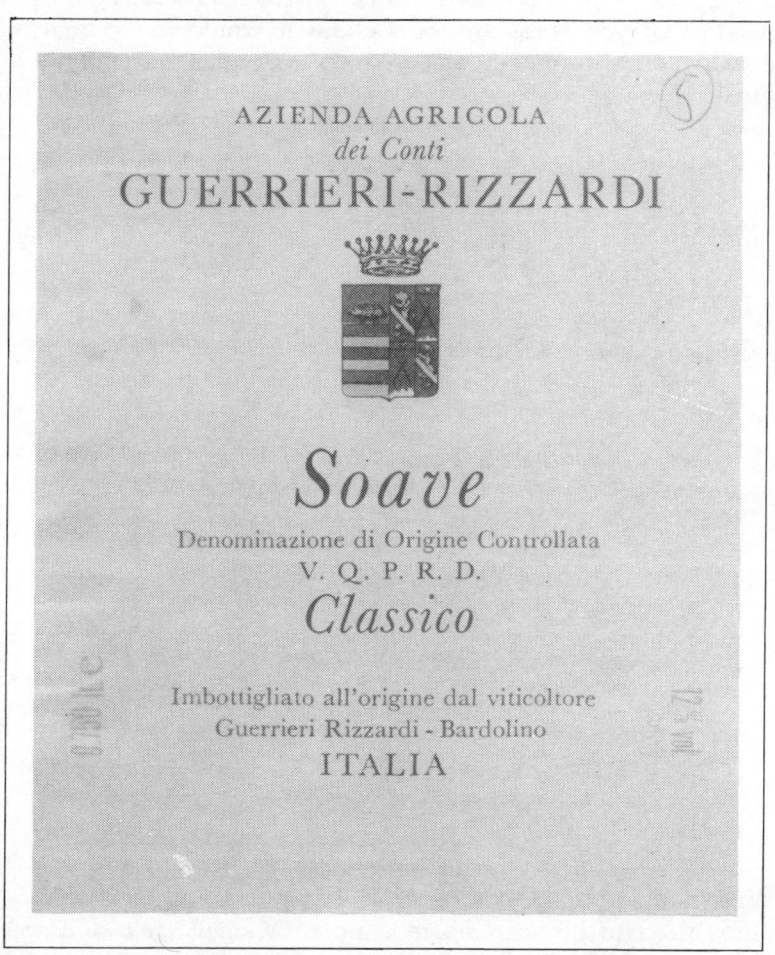

'86 This had a clean, light nose and delicate depth and length with lots of flavour and very good acidity and fruit. It was, perhaps, a little too young and needed time to settle down.

THE ORGANIC WINE GUIDE

VALPOLICELLA-CLASSICO SUPERIORE. DOC. r

Azienda Agricola dei Conti Guerrieri-Rizzardi, Bardolino, 37011 Verona, VENETO

'84 Pale pink in colour, this had a typical nutty nose and one taster thought there was some "tone" to it. There was a light ripe palate that was fresh and frisky and it would make quality quaffing on a summer picnic. There was a typical bitter almond finish.

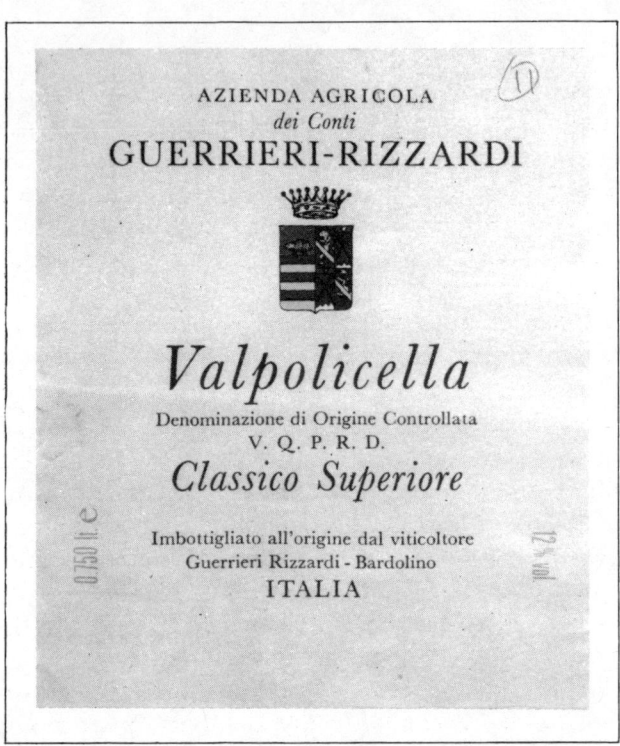

VERNACCIA DI SAN GIMIGNANO. DOC. w

This used to be a favourite wine of Michelangelo and was strong, aged in wood and allowed to develop some oxidised flavours.

'85 There was distinct unanimity on this one; the inside of boots, leather, acetone, toasted, scorched.

SPAIN

The British have an excellent tradition as sherry drinkers. In the mid-16th century a Spanish exporter recorded the equivalent of over two million bottles (4,000 butts) being sent in one year to England. Shakespeare refers to this Spanish wine in *Henry IV Part Two* when Falstaff mentions "Sherris Sack". The name sherry came into use around 1600 as an anglicised version of the city port of Jerez de la Frontera, and as with Burgundy or Champagne, it need not be prefixed with its country, as must the imitators, British or Cyprus sherry types.

The other best-known Spanish wines are those from Rioja in the north, from Pendeñes in Catalonia, south-west of Barcelona, and Valdepeñas in the central plain. The traditional heavy reds have become more refined of late, losing the slight oxidisation that is so acceptable in sherry, and some lovely quality red and white wines are produced.

Spain has yet to feel the full benefit in her wine trade of joining the EEC on 1st January 1986; firstly, she must limit production and distil excesses into brandy (no great problem) or alcohol and has secondly had to abandon rebates to exports regarded as unallowable subsidies. Prices have gone up, but Spanish wine is still generally very good value.

The climate tends to be hot and dry, rather like inland California, and much less variable than in France. Spain produces even less wine per hectare than most organic producers, an average of 20 hectolitres per hectare, several times less than that of an ordinary French producer. This is

THE ORGANIC WINE GUIDE

mainly because traditional farming methods are employed and production is also in many places totally unmodernised; for instance, "tinajas", large clay vats, are still being used for fermentation and vines grow over the ground instead of being staked. Also, low-producing varieties of grape are widely found.

The only organic wine we know of produced in Spain comes form the hot central plain, Valdepeñas in La Mancha region (land of Don Quixote) and is certified as organic by the Vida Sana Association who are a member of IFOAM (International Federation of Organic Agricultural Movements) and therefore adhere to their general principles. A translation of their certifying stamp reads: "A Natural Product: this guarantees the

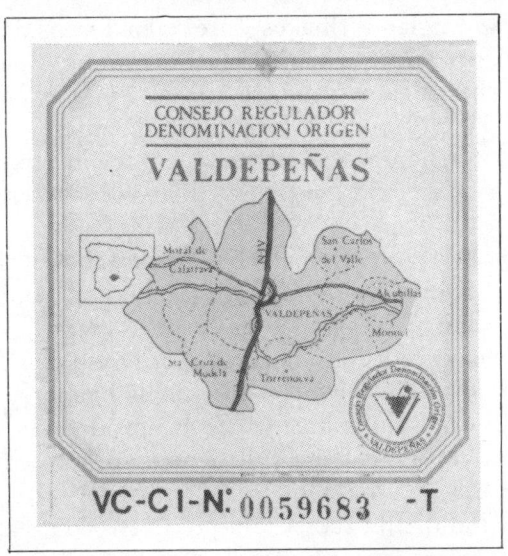

product whose raw materials have been obtained respecting the natural rhythms. Its elaboration has been made without the medication and without the addition of artificial substances, according to the notebook of norms published by the Association.

SPAIN

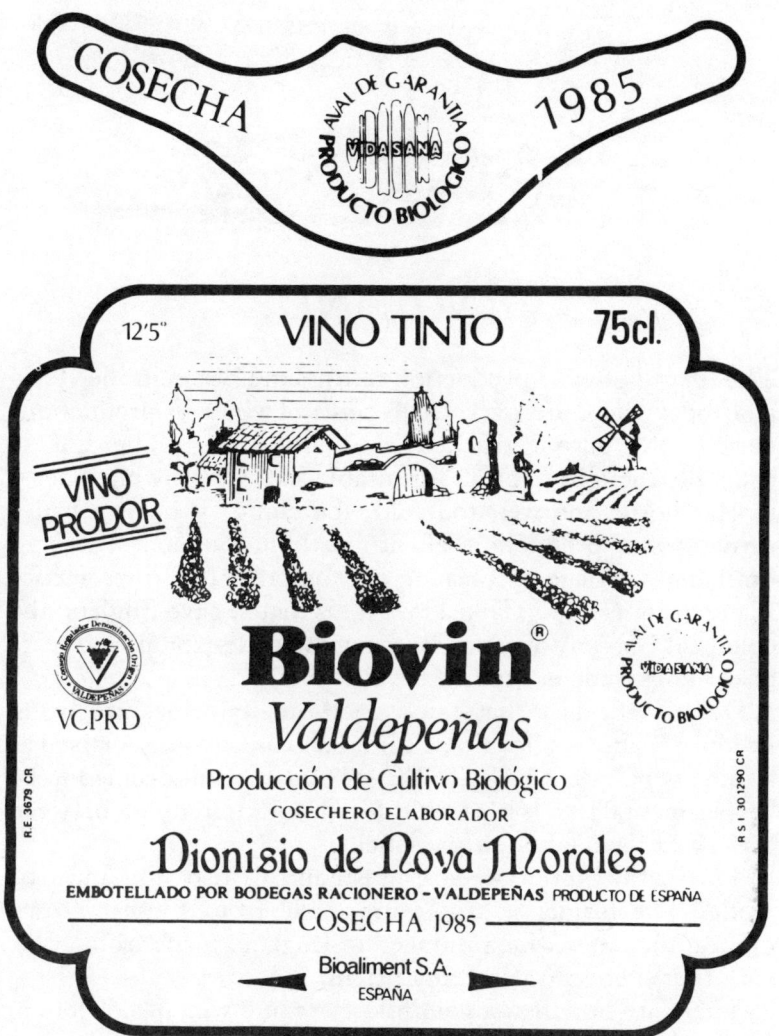

VALDEPEÑAS 1985 VINO TINTO COSECHA (VINTAGE)
Bodegas Racionero, Valdepeñas, Spain

A deep red with a full fruity nose, warm, rich and balanced, nicely round in the mouth, dry with no tannin and a good finish – more sophisticated than expected.

ENGLAND

The revival of wine production in England began in the 1950s and today there are over 1,000 acres of vines in production, nearing the output reached in Tudor times. The UK is generally thought to be an unsuitable area for growing vines – too far north, too wet, too cold, too cloudy – but we had a thriving wine production, albeit mostly in the monasteries up until the marriage of Eleanor of Aquitaine to Prince Henry Plantagenet (Henry II) in 1152. This match gave England the colony of Gascony of which Bordeaux was the capital; 300 years of thriving trade ensued.

Despite the fact that some good-quality wines are being produced, almost all white, all English wine must be classed as "Table wine" according to EEC law, as it is still deemed to be "experimental", so it is as yet difficult to differentiate between the wines for quality on the label.

The distinction between English and British wine must be made. The former is true wine made from English-grown grapes, the latter wine produced in England made from grape (or other) concentrate of any origin.

There are less than a handful of organic wine-producers in England, and those that do exist are all certified by the Soil Association and so carry their symbol. Soil Association standards are based on the standards drawn up by IFOAM, the International Federation of Organic Agricultural Movements, also used by over 40 other member countries in their individual organisations. They also certify (unlike the French and German wine standard organisations) all other types of organic

ENGLAND

agriculture possible, and produce much literature, including a quarterly review, so anyone interested in growing organically, whether vines or simply a personal plot of vegetables, should get in touch. The Soil Association, 86 Colston Street, Bristol, BS1 5BB.

One has to be brave to set out to produce English wine, and even braver to do it organically; these wines are far better than we expected and certainly merit more attention than they get. Everyone on the tasting panel was very pleasantly surprised by the high quality of the English organic wines we tasted.

AVALON
Soil Association
Dr H. R. Howard Tripp, The Drove, East Pennard, Shepton Mallet, Somerset

THE ORGANIC WINE GUIDE

The vineyard was started on a small scale (½ acre) in 1981 and is now about four acres. It has been fully organic since 1984, although they have never used herbicides or fungicides. Weed control is by black polythene mulch. A grass sward, which is mown, is allowed to grow everywhere else, the mowings being left to be recycled by earthworms. Wood ash from burnt prunings and firewood is applied to boost the potash in the spring. Rock phosphate is also used where it is deficient.

So far the wine has been made from seyval grapes (being a hybrid they are resistant to mildew) and recently Dr Tripp has planted Schonburger. Botrytis has been a problem with a heavy crop and a wet autumn. He cuts it out by hand (a laborious process which loses a lot of grapes), caring more for quality than quantity. Strawberries and garlic are grown between the vines and organic cider is also produced.

English Table Wine '85 Almost colourless it was so pale, a leafy gooseberry nose and a lemony flavour; "just the wine for summer picnics" and "best drunk well chilled" were two comments.

CHEVELSWARD
Soil Association
Mrs Ruth Daltry, Chevel House, South Kilworth, Lutterworth, Leicestershire

Mrs Daltry planted her vines of Muller Thurgau in 1973 and had her first small crops in 1976. The next (largest) one was in 1983 when she produced 900 bottles using Roy Cook of Sedlescombe Vineyard to vinify the wine. She doesn't sell it, and reports that it is a dry white wine of which there are only 83 bottles left!

SEDLESCOMBE VINEYARD
Soil Association
Roy and Irma Cook, Robertsbridge, E. Sussex

ENGLAND

This vineyard, originally called Pine Ridge, is by far the largest organic vineyard in England, with 10 acres of vines. It was the first to be approved by the Soil Association, and has been producing organic wine since 1983, having first planted in 1979. The Cooks also import organic German wine and Roy has written some very interesting notes on his tours of German organic vineyards, not to mention his *Vines 'n' Wines Organically*, a self-guided vineyard trail and walk in the woods for the interested visitor. It sounds enormous fun.

They were influenced by a German book called *The Organic Vineyard* and good experiences growing vegetables organically, and they still undercrop almost an acre with strawberries.

As there are no indigenous vines in England the Cooks experiment with early-ripening German varieties (which produce fruit here towards the end of October) and in their vinification they use a 1912 Vertical Basket Press imported from Germany where it had been in use since 1981. It works by pumping a hydraulic fluid down the pipe to the sump at the base of the press which pushes the plunger up through the basket thus pressing the "maische". The juice runs through the channels between the oak slats which make up the basket. After pressing (four hours) there is a dry cake of pips, skins and stalks left to be used as fertiliser in the vineyard.

Sedlescombe Gewurztraminer
Tasters noted an elderflower nose and palate, rosewater flavour, mild spicy taste and an overtone of cloves.

Sedlescombe Gutenbohrer
This grape is a cross between Muller Thurgau and Chasselas Napoléon. The wine was very well received, well balanced with a tart crispish finish. Tasters noted greengages, and high-toned violets.

Sedlescombe Muller Thurgau
A clean nose, rather acidic, but with spritzig and fresh tanginess. A light wine, probably best drunk young.

THE ORGANIC WINE GUIDE

Sedlescombe Reichensteiner

A new variety, popular in England and Muller Thurgau-based, this wine had a lively nose and was very fruity, a tangy, spicy mouthful, dry and crisp. Well liked by everyone.

SWITZERLAND

After several tries we received a list of about 40 Swiss organic wine producers from the Research Institute of Biological Husbandry in Switzerland and, just as we did for every other wine producer, we sent them a synopsis of this book, a letter explaining what we were doing and a questionnaire. Not one replied! So information on organic wine from this country will regrettably have to be omitted here. We were amused to see the heading used by the 1987 *Which? Wine Guide* for Switzerland: it reads, "Secretive Wines". Has Roger Voss had the same problem, I wondered! He notes that Swiss wine all appears to be consumed within the country (it is a huge importer) itself, is of high quality and is expensive. If you are a Swiss organic wine-maker reading this, please get in touch!

AUSTRIA

Austrian wine has been covered at some length in the scandals chapter; a pity because that is where it now lives in too many minds. We mention it here because one lonely organic producer has joined the Swiss Research Institute of Biological Husbandry but we have as yet had no wine or information from him.

The lack of supplies of Austrian wine in the UK and the potentially low prices of wine from this origin can only improve its export opportunities, and as Edmund Penning-Rowsell wrote in a recent article in the *Financial Times* there is much to look forward to.

USA

The United States of America are of particular interest in a guide about organic wines because they look set to have a most definitive influence on wine labelling laws, kicking commercial wine producers worldwide into the 21st century and for the first time making consumers really aware about what goes into a bottle of wine other than love, grapes or greed. Already Californian labels, illustrating a typical American desire to know what's what, often contain information such as where the relevant grapes were picked, how they were fermented and when the wine was bottled, not to mention if the producer used his own grapes or bought them in and trusted to the expert grape-grower.

In 1980 the Bureau of Alcohol, Tobacco and Firearms (BATF), an off-shoot of the Treasury Department, put forward a proposal that had taken nine years to draft – "alcoholic beverages should either: list their ingredients or give an address where consumers could write to obtain a listing". This straightforward requirement was projected to become law by 1983, but the Reagan Administration had it trodden underfoot by 1981 and then tried to abolish the organisation (BATF) that had proposed it. Industry reaction had been explosive and labelled the pro-labellists "neo-prohibitionist"; one argument was that ingredient listing would be too complicated, there were so many! BATF had, as the regulating body, approved more than 100 chemicals and additives for use in wine production. The Reagan Administration announced, under heavy pressure from an industry unhappy about the uphill battle not to lose the sales they foresaw, that "we are unable to conclude that the benefits to the consumer of ingredient labelling for alcoholic beverages outweigh the costs that would be passed on to them as a result of the labelling requirement". The fact that each vintage of wine requires a new label anyway (if only to state the year) was ignored, but the fact that "benefits" to the consumer were identified was a slip in the right direction.

The wine industry in Europe as well as America argues that the mystique of wine-drinking would disappear if the label read like an exam question in chemistry. To put it more bluntly, as Charles Hawkins of Hawkins and Nurrock did, no wine-lover wants his enjoyment ruined by having ox-blood powder printed on the label. Quite right! Let's miss it out of the bottle too, or at least think twice about putting it there in the first place. Such legislation would make wine-makers think carefully about their recipes – something they have perhaps forgotten to do. In the long hot summer of '86 some Burgundy producers, so conditioned to adding sugar to increase their alcohol content, failed to notice the natural intervention and tipped in the sugar regardless. Some very jammy wine was produced in what could have been an outstanding year.

Labelling regulations or not, the American wine-producing industry has in the last 40-odd years gone through a remarkable transition. There are more species of vines native to North America than any other continent. The first English colonists tried to make wine from the wild grapes they found growing there, but failed from lack of enough natural sugar in the grape juice to induce fermentation. When a similar effort was made with imported vines, failure was met again as the grapes could not thrive in such alien conditions and on land infested with *phylloxera*.

For a thirsty immigrant – much of whose food was preserved by thirst-inducing salt – this was more of a problem than it might appear, as "fresh" water was often undrinkable, even poisonous. Early beer-making experiments were also unproductive and brews were more successful in some cases with pumpkins, persimmons, maple sugar or, most commonly, apples. Cider drinking was heavy and widespread. Let us not forget rum either – 18th-century Americans, just before the War of Independence, drank three gallons per head per year, women and children included!

In 1780 *vitis labrusca* (*labrusca* means wild grape) was at last domesticated and became widely planted; by 1840, 15 different states were producing wine, the most prolific being New York, Ohio and Missouri. The wine, however, has a peculiar flavour – commonly called "foxy" – which defies any real subtlety or complexity. A wine-maker in Ohio, Nicholas Longworth, made his fortune from this unfortunate taste. He discovered that it was effectively masked if the wine was sparkling and in the mid-19th century he farmed 1,200 acres near Cincinnati, producing the fashionably sparkling wine, Catawba. The "foxy" taste is created by the chemical methyl anthranilate which only occurs in wines made from lambrusca grapes or hybrids using lambrusca as a cross, contrary to general perception. There are many other native American varieties, Riparia, Aestivalis, Bourguiniana and Rupestris, which do not have this unfortunate taste and many new French/American hybrids have been produced using them – Elvira, Delawares, Concords, Duchess and Diamond.

At about the same time as *vitis labrusca* was being planted in the East, in the far more Mediterranean climate of California a Franciscan monk, Father Junipero Serra, planted what was probably California's first vineyard in 1769. By the mid-19th century many other European grape varieties had been imported to this ideal climate, the influential Agostan Haraszthy having introduced thousands of new cuttings from Europe. The industry flourished, as did immigration during the Gold Rush, and in 1900 no less than 36 medals were awarded to Californian wine in the Paris Exposition.

California experienced the same devastation as French vineyards in the 1860s from *phylloxera* and used the same grafting process to remedy the destruction. No sooner had the vineyards been replanted than Prohibition in 1920 hit the industry for six. It almost died off making only sacramental wine and grape juice – US labelling was on the ball then also, the juice being labelled: "Caution – do not add yeast or the contents will ferment". After Prohibition ended in 1933 this slump had the same long-term beneficial effect as *phylloxera* had in Europe. On replanting vineyards a modern approach was adopted by careful laying out of vines, using better varieties of grape and up-to-date technology, and this provided the foundation of today's high-quality wine production in California.

In modern post-Prohibition USA almost every state has its vineyards (Alaska being the exception). Almost 90% of total production, however, comes from California, from a region stretching over 600 miles. Growers are having great success with traditional French varieties of grapes. Chardonnay and Sauvignon Blanc in particular for whites and Cabernet Sauvignon and Pinot Noir for red wine, although Zinfandel, a native variety, is an interesting one to look for.

The emphasis here is different from European wine production; the pedigree of American wine lies in the truly individual pioneering spirit and confidence of Americans. They believe they can produce whichever wines they want – designer wine in the truest sense (forget the latest trend in rosés called "Blush" wine – that's designers gone overboard!). Enormous back-up comes from the University of Davis in California's Department of Viticulture and Ecology which provides data and information in a way quite lacking in Europe. So in the 1980s Californian wines have lost their early roughness and have become eminently sophisticated. The 1987 *Which? Wine Guide* puts it in a nutshell: they point out that the time is right to buy Californian wines for which prices for good wines have stayed static (unlike France) – "we should all be trying the exciting flavours of wines whose new pursuit of elegance suggests they have come of age".

So, one asks, where are the organic wines in the USA? The easy answer is that they don't exist! Organic is not an acceptable term for wine in the USA. The word "natural" is used, interestingly enough, as it indicates that other wines are not natural. The organisation, California Certified Organic Farmers, will certify a vineyard adhering to their rules and in other areas similar organisations exist. We reproduce a label on p. 182 from Frey Natural Wines to illustrate the different description of organically grown grapes in natural wine, and the

THE ORGANIC WINE GUIDE

use of section 26509.11 of the California Health and Safety Code to authorise it.

CALIFORNIA CERTIFIED ORGANIC FARMERS

California Certified Organic Farmers (CCOF) is an organization formed to promote natural foods and farming without the use of potentially harmful synthetic fertilizers, herbicides or pesticides. CCOF growers achieve insect and weed control by careful timing of cultural practices and using beneficial predators, natural sprays, scientific soil analysis and composting. All strive to maintain a healthy soil – the prerequisite for healthy plants.

To certify a farm under CCOF and the California Organic Food Act (section 26569.11 of the California Health and Safety Code), growers must follow a rigorous soil analysis and ferility program. The CCOF seal is your guarantee of a pure, naturally grown product.

As of early 1987 all US wines must put "contains sulfites" (*sic*) on their labels if they do. There is only one so far which doesn't have to – the Paul Thomas Winery in Washington State prints "contains no sulfites" on one of its wines and is justifiably proud to say (we are) "the first American Winery to demonstrate that it can make wine without use of sulfur and prove this in lab testing" (by the FDA). The wine was also produced organically. As an interesting note this same wine has won a trade blind tasting as the best blush (rosé) Zinfandel – and it is made from rhubarb, organically grown, of course!

FOUR CHIMNEYS' FARM WINERY
New York State Natural Food Associates, RD1 Hall Road, Himrod on Seneca, New York. 14842

On the west shore of Lake Seneca Four Chimneys' château and barn were built during the Civil War in the Italianate villa style. A structure known as the Grape House, once used to keep the harvested grapes out of the sun until they were put on barges bound for the Erie Canal and beyond now serves as owner Walter Pedersen's residence. He bought it in 1976, although table grapes have been grown here since 1870, and now farms 12 acres of vines organically, using manure, compost and seaweed, herbal and vegetable sprays and hay or straw mulches to control weeds. Periodically large quantities of beneficial

USA

insect predators such as ladybirds and lacewings are introduced to aid insect control; clover is the chief green manure cover crop and good soil management has negated the need for chemical bacterial and fungal sprays. Unusually, Walter Pedersen grows a wide variety of grapes not otherwise found in New York State – Gamay, Chenin Blanc and Johannesburg Riesling, along with Cabernet Sauvignon and Pinot Noir. This wine list includes the following: Primeur Nouveau Red, Red Table Wine, Kingdom White, Kingdom Red (Special Reserve), Riesling, Johannesburg Riesling, Late Harvest Delaware, Chardonnay, Cabernet Sauvignon and Dayspring.

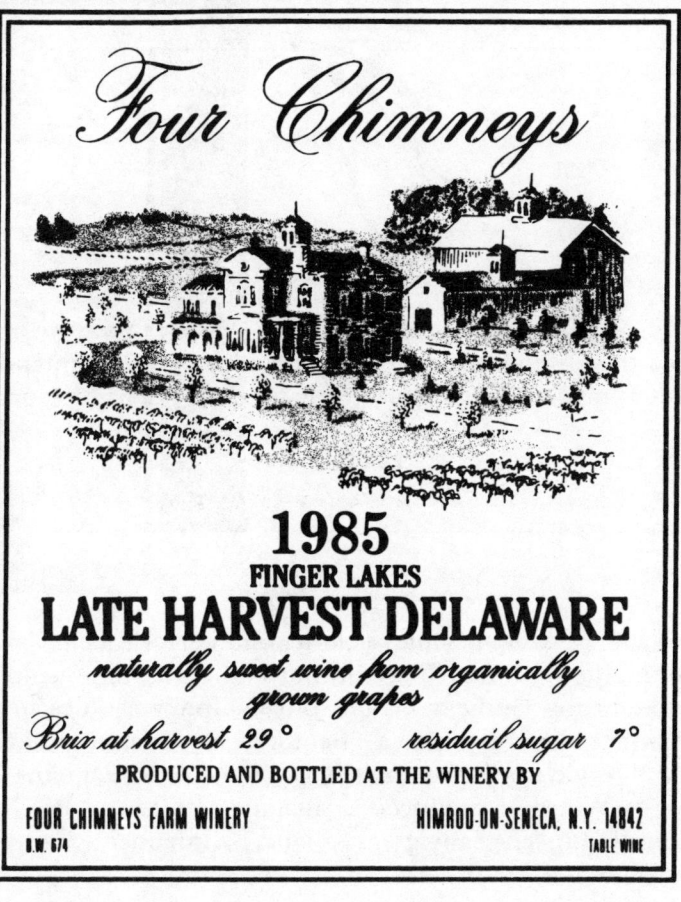

THE ORGANIC WINE GUIDE

FREY NATURAL WINES
14000 Tomki Road, Redwood Valley, California. 95470

Situated on the slopes at the foot of Tomki Canyon, this vineyard has an ideal micro-climate for wine-growing. The vineyards, at an elevation of 1,000 feet, are managed in accordance with California Certified Organic Farmers' Standards. Careful traditional techniques, such as punching down the red

wine caps, racking to achieve clarity and barrel-ageing, create definitive local wines. They do not add sorbates or sulphur dioxide during vinification, but burn sulphur candles in the barrels (a traditional practice). Bentonite clay is used as a fining agent. The yield is approximately two tons per acre, giving 900 litres. Wines produced include Grey Riesling, Gewurztraminer, Sauvignon Blanc, Zinfandel, Cabernet Sauvignon and Syrah.

AUSTRALIA

Australia is included in this guide because we anticipate in the not-too-distant future some exciting additions to our *Organic Wine Guide*. There are several producers making what is reckoned to be organic wine, but none as yet has this information printed on the label. More relevant today is that domestic sales of Australian wine do have some form of ingredient labelling, with, in particular, sulphur dioxide stated on bottles as an ingredient. Wine exported into the UK or other markets does not have to comply, so don't automatically assume that a bottle without E220 printed on the label doesn't have it, or has less than one which does, and there are quite a few Australian bottles with E numbers now in circulation, raising eyebrows all round. Australian wine is also an exciting phenomenon in itself; many superb quality individual wines are produced, and the land itself is ideal for this purpose as the south basks in a Mediterranean-type climate, growing European-type vines.

The Australian public has only in the last 20 years developed into a true wine-drinking nation, (although early settlers had much success from the start with wine production, unlike the USA). Now twice as much wine is drunk per person in Australia than in the UK or USA.

JAPAN

Japan is one of the fastest-growing consumer markets for wine. An increase of 50% per annum in consumption in the early 1970s has slowed down to around 15% annually in the mid-1980s. So, for European producers keen to find new export markets Japan is potentially very attractive. The situation is hampered at the moment by several factors, principally excessively high import duties on bottled wines. Hope lies in the promise made by the Japanese Government to review taxes and levies in 1987, and there is some confidence that the position will improve as the government is keen to be seen to please the electorate after recent surprise losses in the polls.

Japan itself produces fairly low-alcohol wine, around 8%-9%, influenced by high rainfall in the summer months. Wine producers attempt to counterbalance this by importing bulk wine and blending it with their own production. It is impossible to tell what percentage is in fact included in a bottle of so-called "Japanese" wine as producers are under no legal remit to state basic facts on the label – not even the producer's name! A large tidying-up of label definitions and descriptions has been mooted, but as yet no decisive action has taken place. Discussions are still being had about whether to drop Champagne as a descriptive term: the French producers must hope that this will be achieved without the same lengthy and expensive legal action they had to submit to to keep the Spaniards in line.

Meanwhile Japanese wine producers take cool advantage of the lower import tax on bulk wine; blended product still retails

JAPAN

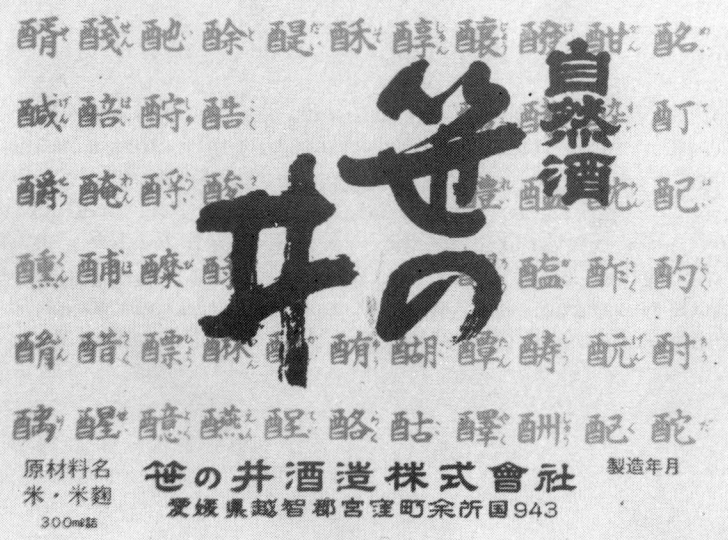

THE ORGANIC WINE GUIDE

at an unnecessarily high premium, with the producer pocketing the difference. The much publicised exorbitant duty on Scottish whisky in Japan has been under a much pressurised (from the EEC and USA) review, and if a sensible price can be achieved on this one hopes wine will follow suit – but with Japan one can never tell!

Enough said. We include this short chapter on Japan, not because of their grape wine (although it is important to give a background) but because there is but one organic wine producer in Japan, making – you guessed it – sake. We would argue that in fact the only wine of real interest in Japan today is the traditional Sake rice wine, and Akadana, a plum wine.

SASANOI GYOZO are a third-generation organic wine-producing family based in South Island, manufacturing their wine from organic brown rice (most sake is made from white) including 30% of the grain's hull (skin) as it is difficult to use a koji – the starter yeast – without breaking the hull. To start fermentation, a seed, koji, is added to the mixture every day for three days, adding more rice each time to form a layered structure. The full fermentation period is two months and the family have now changed from using wooden kegs to stainless steel as they experienced problems from unwanted bacteria in the wood, hampering hygiene. No sulphur is added; to achieve sterilisation a long and slow process of passing the wine through a small tube and steaming it is utilised (like pasteurisation), the sake then being stored in large tanks to cool before bottling. Three separate grades of sake are produced, the top quality being the highest in alcohol content. As yet the produce is regrettably unavailable in the UK, although Real Foods in Edinburgh do stock brown rice sake from time to time and will include the organic sake when it is available. Don't forget, to complete the experience sake should be drunk warm.

DISTRIBUTORS

We include here not only a list of retail outlets where organic wines are sold, but some restaurants who include them on their lists, and we'd be grateful to know of any we have yet to hear of – please fill in the form at the end of the book with your comments and information.

We begin with a list of distributors who supply organic wine wholesale (details at each entry) or by the case to Mail Order or visiting customers. Our special thanks go to those distributors who donated samples, Real Foods, Vintage Roots, Vinceremos, Haughton Fine Wines, Yapp Brothers, Connoisseur Wines, West Heath Wines and Lincolnshire Wine Company.

REAL FOODS TRADING LTD
14 Ashley Place, Edinburgh EH6 5PX, Scotland. tel 031-554-4321. telex 72189

Supply nationwide over 40 organic certified wines (along with an enormous range of natural and organic foods), both also by Mail Order. A separate list is available (send s.a.e.). Deliver in own trucks or by carrier (also two shops in Edinburgh). The largest natural food and wine distributor in Europe, stock everything from organic fruits to Japanese seaweed.

VINTAGE ROOTS
88 Radstock Road, Reading, Berks. RG1 3PR, England. tel 0734-662569.

Sell only organic wines, mostly with certification from Nature

THE ORGANIC WINE GUIDE

et Progrès or other organisations, hope soon to join Soil Association to certify all wines. Minimum order one case (can be mixed); delivery by carrier £2.95. Good list with interesting tasting notes and includes many excellent wines.

HAUGHTON FINE WINES
The Coach House, Haughton, Tarporley, Cheshire. CW6 9RN. tel 0829-261032

Import a selection of fine French wines, including many "Vins Biologique". All wines are estate bottled. By the case or for trade, wines can be sampled at tastings, collected or delivered.

CONNOISSEUR WINES LTD
27 Carnath Road, London SW6 3HR. tel 01-736-9727
Stock three organic wines (amidst a wide list) from Provence.

LES BONS VINS OCCITANS
19a Wetherby Gardens, London SW5. tel 01-370-6529

Lavinia Gibbs-Smith lives mostly in France and stocks a good range of 27 organic wines amongst others for UK distribution. She also holds wine tastings and provides information on other wine events.

VINCEREMOS
Beechwood Centre, Elmete Lane, Leeds LS8 2LQ. tel 0532-734056

An unusual list from far-flung places, including USSR, Zimbabwe and Cuba! Stock 16 organic wines from France, England and Spain. Express delivery (at a cost) or otherwise anywhere by the case. All organic wines certified by Nature et Progrès or others.

SEDLESCOMBE VINEYARD
Robertsbridge, E. Sussex. tel 058083-715

Stock their own organic wine, plus a few from Germany. An interesting place to visit.

DISTRIBUTORS

WEST HEATH WINE
Pirbright, Surrey. GU24 0QE. tel 04867-6464

All Andrew Williams' wines are approved by Nature et Progrès. He stocks a variety of French, which can be delivered free in London, or elsewhere with carriage charge.

C. C. G. EDWARDS
Shillingstone, Dorset. DT11 0SP. tel 0258 860641

Stocks South of France and German organic wines, also fruit juice, olive oil and honey.

THE LINCOLNSHIRE WINE CO.
Chapel Lane, Ludborough, Nr Grimsby DN36 5SJ. tel 0472-840858

A list of exclusively German organic wines.

THE ORGANIC WINE CO. LTD
P.O. Box 81, High Wycombe, Buckinghamshire. HP11 1LJ

A range of French and German organic wines.

YAPP BROTHERS LTD
Mere, Wiltshire. BA12 6DY. tel 0747-860423

An excellent list of wines, with a few organic inclusions tucked in.

ORGANIC WINE STOCKISTS

LONDON and SOUTH-EAST

Arjuna Ltd, Unit 7, Dales Brewery, Gwydir Street, Cambridge CB1 2AD
The Beer Shop, 8 Pitfield Street, London N1
Bennett & Luck, 54 Islington Park Street, London N1
Bon Appétit, 2 North Parade Avenue, Oxford
Brampton's of Salisbury, 21 Queen Street, Salisbury, Wilts.
Clearspring Grocers, 196 Old Street, London E1
Cook's Delight, 360 High Street, Berkhamsted, Herts.
Cooper's Natural Foods, 17 Lower Marsh Street, London W5
Cornucopia Wholefoods, 64 St Mary's Road, Ealing, London W5
The Cromer Kitchen, 3 Church Street, Cromer, Norfolk. NR27 9ER
Curzon Wine Company, 11 Curzon Street, London W1
Di's Larder, 62 Lavender Hill, London SW11
Fleming's Wines, 31 Forehill, Ely, Cambs.
The Garland Wine Cellar, 20 Craddocks Parade, Ashtead Surrey. KT21 1QJ
Garland's Farm Organic Shop, Garland's Farm, Upper Basildon, Nr Reading, Berks.
Gateways Wholefoods, 21 The Borough, Canterbury, Kent
Gerald Harris Wine Shop, Aston Clinton, Buckinghamshire
German Food Centre, Knightsbridge, London
Gluttons Delicatessen, 110 Walton Street, Oxford
Grape Hive Wines, 392a Chiswick High Road, London W4
The Ground Floor, 27 Endell Street, London WC2

STOCKISTS

Hargun's Food Store, 14 Cholmeley Road, Reading, Berks.
Harvest Foods, 12 St John's Street, Colchester, Essex
Hay Wholefoods & Deli, Lion Street, Hay-on-Wye, Herefordshire
Infinity Foods Co-op Ltd, 25 North Road, Brighton, Sussex
The Jug & Firkin, 90 Mill Road, Cambridge
La Réserve, 56 Walton Street, London SW3
La Vigneronne, 105 Old Brompton Road, London SW7
Nut-Trux, Unit 8, Park Royal Business Centre, 17-19 Park Royal Road, London NW10
Oliver's Wholefood Shop, 243 Munster Road, Fulham, London
The Organic Shop, 120 Ferndale Road, Clapham, London SW4
Peaches Health Foods, 143 High Street, Wanstead, London E11
Peppercorns Granary, 2 Heath Street, Hampstead, London
Pepper's Natural Food, Distributors, 317 Lower High Street, Cheltenham, Gloucestershire
Ravensbourne Wine Co. Ltd, 6.1.13 Bell House, 49 Greenwich High Road, London SE10
Stores of Belgravia, 6 Port Street, London SW1
Richmond Wine Warehouse, 138c Lower Mortlake Road, Richmond, Surrey. TW9 2JZ
Sunstore Wholefood Shop, Marsh Lane, Newbury, Berks. RG13 1HS
Wholefoods, 31 Paddington Street, London W1
Wild Oats, 146 Sea Road, Angmering-on-Sea, West Sussex
C. J. Wilkmin, Jordan's Courtyard, 8 Upper High Street, Thame, Oxfordshire
Windmill Wholefoods, 486 Fulham Road, London SW6

LONDON AND SOUTH-EAST HOTELS AND RESTAURANTS
The Bagatelle, Chipping Campden, Glos.
The Dining Room, Winchester Wald, Bedale Street, London SE1

THE ORGANIC WINE GUIDE

SOUTH-WEST
Ambassador Wines, 7 High Street, Yeovil, Somerset
Carley & Co., 35/36 St Austell Street, Truro, Cornwall
Real Ale & Cheese Shop, Bridge House, St Clement's Street, Truro, Cornwall
"Seasons", 10 George Street, Bath, Avon
Widcombe Wine, 12 Widcombe Parade, Cloverton Street, Bath, Avon

SOUTH-WEST RESTAURANTS
Wild Oats II, Vegetarian Restaurant, 85 Whiteladies Road, Bristol, Avon

MIDLANDS
Arkwrights, Louth, Lincs.
Broad Bean Wholefoods, 60 Broad Street, Ludlow, Salop
F.O.E. One Earth Shop, 54 Alison Street, Birmingham, W. Midlands
Good Earth, 17 Free Lane, Leicester
Health & Wholefoods, Sleaford, Lincs.
Health Food Store, 41 Oxford Road, Altrincham, Cheshire
Hiziki Wholefoods, 15 Goosegate, Hockley, Nottingham
Horncastle Wholefoods, Horncastle, Lincs.
Mitchell's Wine Merchants, Victoria Centre, 29-33 Knifesmithgate, Chesterfield
Moden's, Spilsby, Lincs.
National Centre for O/G Gardening, Ryton-on-Dunsmore, Coventry
Natural Choice, 31 Hope Street, Hanley, Stoke-on-Trent, Staffordshire
The Stores, Baschurch, Salop
The Stores, North Thoresby, Lincolnshire
The Stores, South Elkington, Lincs.
Tate's Supermarket, Grimsby, Lincs.
Witham Wines, Lincoln, Lincs.

MIDLANDS RESTAURANTS AND HOTELS
The Abbey Green Vegetarian Restaurant, Chester, Cheshire
The Bailiwick, Top Farm, Farndon, Cheshire

STOCKISTS

Delany's Vegetarian Restaurant, Wyle Cop, Shrewsbury, Salop
The Epworth Tap, Epworth, Lincs.

THE NORTH
The Ale House, 79 Raglan Road, Leeds LS2
Bear Wholefoods Co-operative, 17 Water Street, Todmorden, Lancs. OL14 5AB
Cairns & Hickey, 17 Blenheim Terrace, Leeds 2
The Dram Shop, 21 Commonside, Sheffield
Hopkins Porter, Ripley Castle Shop, Ripley Castle, Nr Harrogate, N. Yorks
IVC Co-op. Ltd, Peel Industrial Centre, Peel Road West, Pimbo, Skelmersdale, Lancs. WN8 9PT
Kan Foods, 29 Kirkland, Kendal, Cumbria
Legendary Lancashire Heroes, 62 Burton Road, Withington
Lewis & Cooper, Market Place, Northallerton, N. Yorks.
Mitchell's Wine Merchant, 354 Meadowhead, Sheffield, S. Yorks.
Natural Choice, 2 Market Place, Polton-le-Fylde, Nr Blackpool, Lancs.
Natureway, 122 Harrogate Road, Chapel Allerton, Leeds 7
Open Sesame, 2 High Street, Sedgefield, Co. Durham
The Shepherd's Purse, Church Street, Whitby
Single Step Co-op., 76a Penn Street, Lancaster
The York Beer Shop, 28 Sandringham Street, York

THE NORTH RESTAURANTS AND HOTELS
Billie's Vegetarian Restaurant, Chorlton, Manchester
The Coach House, Crookham, Cornhill-on-Tweed, Northumberland
The Deansgate, Manchester
The Granary Restaurant, Grimsby, Humberside
The Greenhouse Restaurant, 331 Great Western Street, Rusholme, Manchester M14 4AN
The Hoi Tin, Warrington, Durham
Lancrigg Vegetarian Hotel, Easedale, Grasmere
The Village Bakery, Melmerby, Penrith, Cumbria

THE ORGANIC WINE GUIDE

SCOTLAND
Bean Machine, Barnhills Farm, Near Denholm, Roxburghshire
Caledonian Stores, Corpach, Fort William
Donaldson's, 3 High Street, Aberdour, Fife
Millstone, 15 High Street, Oban
Nastiuks, 10 Gillespie Place, Edinburgh
Judith Paris, The Vaults, 4 Giles Street, Leith, Edinburgh
Peckham & Rye, 21 Clarence Drive, Hyndland, Glasgow
Peppermint HF House, 247b St John's Road, Corstorphine, Edinburgh
Peter Green, 37a/b Warrender Park Road, Edinburgh
Real Foods, 8 Brougham Street, Tollcross, Edinburgh
Real Foods, 37 Broughton Street, Edinburgh EH1
Quinn's Grain Store, 229/235 Argyle Street, Glasgow
Paul Sanderson Wines, 67/69 Main Street, Davidsons Mains, Edinburgh
The Wine Shop, 7 Sinclair Street, Caithness
The Wine Well, 3 Chambers Street, Edinburgh EH1
Valvona & Crolla, 19 Elm Row, Edinburgh

SCOTLAND RESTAURANTS AND HOTELS
Argyll Hotel, Fiona Menzies, Isle of Iona, Argyll
Country Kitchen, 2 City Road, Brechin, Angus
Country Kitchen, 2 Lochland Street, Arbroath, Angus
La Marché Noir Restaurant, Eyre Place, Edinburgh
La Potinière, Gullane, East Lothian
Martin's Restaurant, Rose Street Lane North, Edinburgh
The Shore Restaurant & Bar, The Shore, Leith, Edinburgh

WALES
RESTAURANTS AND HOTELS
The Cross Lanes Hotel, Marchwell, Clwyd

FOOD AND WINE

As opposed to wine with food! Question: Why eat it when you can drink it? Answer: Because it's the easiest way in the world to produce delicious food, and when you have worked your way through as many bottles of organic wine as we have if we didn't cook with it we'd drown . . . . The added bonus, of course, is that you can tipple while you cook, so that no matter how your food turns out you are in a marvellous mood!

Please don't be put off by the cost, the worst wine open for days and going a touch vinegary can at a pinch be turned into excellent sauces. Remember that a squeeze of lemon or a touch of vinegar itself is often all that you need to transform fish or mayonnaise, not that we're recommending using only low-quality wine – quite the contrary – just don't overlook it.

Strongly flavoured sauces have traditionally been used to flavour bland, carbohydrate foods such as rice, wheat or grain-based dishes, and some of the best-known ethnic condiments – shoyu soy sauce, spices and curries are used in every meal. So by using wine you can really transform a very cheap meal rather than following the rich habits of the West and only adding alcoholic flavour to meat or fish.

Still on the subject of expense, consider what you might spend on a night out for two with a bottle of overpriced wine and two brandies. I get disillusioned eating food that I could easily cook far better myself. So I do, at a fraction of the price, and don't stint on the wine.

We include some of our own favourite recipes in this book in the hope that you'll enjoy the experience of producing them, and also in the hope that if you have not already done so you will now turn from organic wine to organic food. Change the world – you have to start somewhere!

RECIPES

LEEKS IN OIL a WHITE WINE

When I was a student in Birmingham my sister's godfather, Harlan Walker, and his wife Delia introduced me to a new world of food, and this method of cooking leeks is an adaptation of one Harlan taught me. He included small tomatoes cut in half which my husband spurns with true macrobiotic disdain (related to the deadly nightshade – poisonous!)

Clean as large a bunch of leeks as you can eat (remember they always end up as less than you think) and chop into one-inch lengths, separating the layers of larger chunks. Using a heavy pan with a lid, toss the leeks with a good oil (I prefer cold-pressed safflower) and pour on about a cup of wine (for say 2lb of leeks), no other liquid. Cook slowly over a low heat, lid on tight, for about 20 minutes, until the leeks are soft and starting to go brown on the bottom. I prefer to eat with (organic USA) brown rice to offset the delicious oily cooking liquid, and simple fish. Good additions to this dish during cooking are sliced mushrooms, tofu or broccoli.

Don't forget that organic leeks are far superior in flavour and happily can be found in natural food shops and supermarkets when in season.

MUSHROOMS EN MEURETTE

When baskets of mushrooms suddenly become plentiful and can be bought for the same price that usually pays for a half-pound we eat this delicious simple stew by the bowlful – usually accompanied by brown rice, millet or bulghar to soak up the excess juice.

Lightly fry the mushrooms in oil (butter, of course, is fine but I rarely use it for cooking – we love oil and keep perhaps eight different kinds on the kitchen worktop). Remove the mushrooms and add a generous dose of roughly chopped garlic cloves and a finely chopped onion (one large one or several small), stir in a tablespoon of flour, lightly brown then add a

FOOD AND WINE

pint of red wine. Reduce the mixture to a rich smooth sauce, adding a couple of bay leaves and whichever fresh herbs you like or have but for preference parsley, and a good grind of black pepper. This can take up to half-an-hour. Add the mushrooms back in, simmer for a further five minutes and serve.

This dish is also delicious cold, with bread to dip in the sauce – if I've made a lot, a quick blend in a food processor makes great soup. Stir in a dollop of sheep's yoghurt.

HERRINGS IN WINE AND HERBS

This is such an easy recipe, and is first-rate served hot or cold. I use two herrings per person, or one for children (not suitable for the under-fives as the odd fish-bone always turns up).

Buy filleted herring, lay flat and add a generous dollop, about two tablespoons, of a mixture roughly chopped in or out of a food processor of the following: One large onion, two cored apples, a bunch of fresh parsley, 2oz butter, ground black pepper. Roll up the fish, place in a well-oiled dish, pour over two cups of white wine and cover with foil and bake in a medium to slow oven for 45 minutes. (As an Aga cook I use the top of the bottom oven).

BONED CHICKEN WITH MANGOES AND SWEETBREADS

1 chicken
1 lb calves' or lambs' sweetbreads
1 lb pork
1 or 2 mangoes
bread
1 egg

People are invariably impressed when presented with a boned stuffed chicken or duck. The most difficult thing about boning a chicken is getting started because it does seem a daunting task. I would suggest getting a book with illustrated instructions, a small sharp knife, and just doing it. There are two methods – in one you cut along the backbone and in the other you work through the vents. I prefer the latter.

Once the deed is done, prepare the stuffing by blanching and de-membraning the sweetbreads (calves' are best and less bother), peel the mango and cut into large pieces, then mince the pork and bread. Put the pork, breadcrumbs and any pieces of chicken into a mixing-bowl and work in the egg and season. Working from both ends, stuff the bird with mixture and the sweetbreads and mango so that they are evenly distributed and sew up the vents. Massage the bird into a good shape, paint with melted butter and roast in the middle of a medium oven for about an hour and a half. The bird will have resumed its original shape and can be served immediately or used as the centrepiece of a cold buffet. There is a horribly arrogant pleasure in asking someone to carve.

Italian Cream Sauce
    1 pint double cream
    packet of dried mushrooms (porcini)
    1/4lb boiled ham

This recipe is disgustingly simple and delicious. Put the cream in a pan, rinse the mushrooms in water and add to the cream and simmer until the cream has reduced by half. If the mushrooms have not fully reconstituted then leave off the heat for 15 minutes or so. Before serving, add the chopped ham and pour over both plain and spinach tagliatelle.

Ox Cheek in Orange
    2lbs ox cheek
    1/2lb carrots
    1/2lb onions
    1/2lb leeks
    garlic
    fresh ginger
    chilli
    1/2 pint strong white wine
    1/2 pint orange juice

Try to buy the cheek in a piece so you can cut it up for yourself, but failing that try to get big chunks and be ruthless about trimming away the membrane. Roughly chop the vegetables and fry in oil and butter and when just softened throw in some finely chopped garlic, ginger and chilli for a little lift. Remove the vegetables, add more oil and brown the meat. Return the the vegetables, sprinkle with a little flour, stir and add the wine and orange juice.

    Cover and simmer for about two hours and when the meat is

tender remove it with a slotted spoon and keep warm. Let the vegetables cool and process to a purée. If it is too thin to nicely coat the meat, quickly reduce it over a high heat and return the meat.

To garnish, take an orange and with a very sharp knife cut away the skin and pith. Hold the orange in one hand and cut out the segments, catching the juice in a bowl underneath, and strew over the meat before serving. Plain pasta or potatoes would be fine with this.

ALSACE CHERRY SOUP (FOR SIX)

1 bottle dry Alsace wine
1lb cherries
1 pint yoghurt or double cream
2 lemons
2oz sugar
piece of cinnamon stick

Stone the cherries with an olive or cherry stoner or with a knife. Crack about a third of the stones with a hammer and put all the stones, stalks, sugar, juice from the two lemons plus the grated rind from one, and the wine into an enamelled pan – aluminium would discolour the wine – and simmer for 15 minutes. Strain through a nylon or plastic sieve, return to pan, add cherries and bring back to boil for a few minutes. Once cool, whisk the liquid into the yoghurt and chill for a couple of hours. Before serving add a teaspoon or so of salt and more lemon juice if required. This soup is a beautiful colour and should be garnished with halved cherries and/or variegated mint.

HUNZA APRICOTS

Years ago, in the early days of Real Foods, we were tickled pink to have Elizabeth David as a Mail Order customer, and I subsequently had several fascinating talks with her on the phone – and once in person – about our food. I remember she was pleased to find that we stocked Hunza apricots as she had been unable to find them for years. Even now we addicts often have to suffer for long periods when none are shipped into the UK. They are small (about one inch in diameter) spherical dried fruit, brownish orange and with the stone still inside. They enlarge by about 50% when soaked. The apricots come from the Hunza Valley, an area in Afghanistan, North Pakistan and the China border. I have long soaked them for breakfast, used them in curries, fruit salads, cakes, ice cream and so on – but this recipe has been one of my favourites. It is my adaptation of one invented by my friend Jane Jones.

Wash, say, a kilo (or any weight) of apricots thoroughly (one of the reasons for the dearth of supplies in the UK is infestation damage which puts importers off – a good sign of no chemicals), then bring to the boil in just enough water to cover the fruit and simmer for only five or ten minutes. I divide the apricots into several batches, perhaps four. Then each batch is bottled with enough left-over sweet wine (or really anything alcoholic we've got and that we don't want to drink – usually the aftermath of a summer holiday) and brandy (or similar) about half and half to well cover them and put safely away to mature. Two years ago I mixed the different bottles in kilner jars and gave them as Christmas presents. The end product is fabulous. Just don't forget to drink the juice!

SLIMMER'S TIPPLE

We eat for a wide variety of different reasons, hunger being lower down the list for many lucky wine-drinkers than they may be willing to admit. Personally I love food and working in the natural food business brings a variety of delicious experiences – every day it seems the postman brings interesting samples of endless new varieties of natural foods from healthy snacks, samples of nuts (pistachios, macadamias) and fruit (muscatel raisins, Hunza apricots) to weird and wonderful flavoured soya drinks or seaweeds – even organic wine!

We nibble on some days quite uncontrollably – usually when the tension is high. The beauty of natural foods is that they contain no added sugar so the waistline – more in danger as one grows older – suffers only minimally, and your average glutton can eat very satisfactorily if he sticks to a healthy diet.

But what about drinking habits? All that designer water is excellent but gets boring and fruit juice, sugar or not, piles on the calories. So what of wine? The tendency of many a happy drinker is to presume that if the wine is white and dry it can be relied upon to minimise the calories. Not so. The alcohol content does by far the most damage, so forget that bone-dry

FOOD AND WINE

tasteless Bordeaux and look towards Germany for something perhaps around 8% alcohol with little or no chaptalisation.

By the end of May 1989 all EEC wines will be required by law to state the alcohol content on the label, but meanwhile it is difficult to judge the alcoholic level if it is not printed because a good southern wine-maker will not necessarily take total advantage of the extra sunshine and let his grapes ripen to provide maximum alcohol – he will often prefer to pick earlier and concentrate on quality instead. Conversely, it is impossible to presume that northern European wines with their cooler climates will be lower in alcohol because of traditional sugar addition.

If in doubt, stick to bottles that state the low alcohol content now – there are many. One final tip. If you are going to limit your alcohol consumption on a diet, try drinking before a meal on an empty stomach for maximum alcoholic stimulation! then have two glasses while you eat; one for thirst-quenching water, the other to sip the wine that offsets the (low-calorie) natural meal you are tucking into.

GLOSSARY

ACETIC ACID: The acid found in vinegar and spoiled wine.
ACIDITY: The tartaric, malic and citric acids found in grapes which give wine a sharpness or edge and help wine keep. If there is not enough acidity wine can be flabby; high acidity goes with age. Acidity in wine can be adjusted chemically.
AGE: Desirable in big reds and whites; undesirable in light wines designed to be refreshing such as some Loire whites.
ALCOHOL: That which gets you drunk; normally expressed on the label in percentage by volume.
ANBAUGEBIETE (Germany): Legally defined region of origin as in Qualitätswein bestimmter Anbaugebiete (QbA) e.g. Rheinhessen.
AUSLESE (Germany): Selected ripe grapes, third highest in QmP class.
BALANCE: The correct amount of both acidity and sweetness in white wine; acidity, fruit and tannin in red.
BEERENAUSLESE (Germany): Selected ripe grapes, late harvested, second highest in QmP class.
BEREICH (Germany): Legally defined subregion. The 11 Qualitätswein regions (Anbaugebiete) have 32 subregions (Bereich) e.g. Bereich Bernkastel.
BLANC DE BLANCS (France): Wine made solely from white grapes.
BLENDING: Assembling wines of different origin and/or age to create a house style, improve faults, etc.
BODY: The "weight" of the wine in the mouth, comprising alcohol and other physical components.
BOTRYTIS: The fungus that produces noble rot or "pourriture

GLOSSARY

noble" which creates the great sweet Sauternes and Trockenbeerenausleses.
BOUQUET: The aroma or nose of a wine.
CARBONIC MACERATION: The method whereby whole uncrushed grapes are put in the fermentation vessel. Those at the bottom, of course, do get crushed and start fermenting, giving off carbon dioxide which forces out the air (carbon dioxide from cylinders is also forced in). The grapes have started fermenting in their own skin then burst and this gives more fruit and colour to the wine. It is used especially for wines made to be drunk young, e.g. Beaujolais, and to a growing extent in the Midi.
CAVE (France): A cellar.
CÉPAGE (France): Grape variety.
CHAIS (France): A building for storing wine.
CHAPTALISATION: The addition of sugar to must before or during fermentation to increase alcohol and weight.
CHÂTEAU: A wine estate, not necessarily having a castle.
CLOS (France): A walled vineyard, often used when walls no longer exist.
COMMUNE (France): A wine-producing village or administrative unit.
CÔTE (France): A slope or hillside, can be small or large area.
CRÉMANT (France): A champagne-style sparkler, commonly from Alsace and Burgundy.
CRU (France): A crop of grapes or a vineyard and its production.
CUVÉ (France): A wine vat.
CUVÉE (France): The contents of a vat or a blended wine.
DECANT: To pour wine into a carafe or decanter, leaving any sediment in the bottle. It also allows the wine to breathe.
DOMAINE (France): An estate or single property.
EINZELLAGE (Germany): A legally defined single vineyard.
ENGRAIS (France): Fertiliser
ESTATE BOTTLED: Can be a guarantee that the wine has not been blended with anything inferior.
FILTRATION: Putting wine through filter to clarify it.
FINING: Clarifying wine with the likes of gelatin, egg whites

and clays which cause particles in suspension to fall to the bottom.

FREE RUN: The juice which comes from grapes before they are pressed.

GROSSLAGE (Germany): A collective site, registered vineyards with similar characteristics.

KABINETT (Germany): The basic class of QmP wines.

LEES: The sediment at the bottom of barrel after fermentation.

MACERATION: Steeping grapes in their own juice before fermentation.

MARC (France): The skin, pips and stalks left after pressing; also spirit fermented from same.

MILDEW: Fungus disease.

MILLÉSIME (France): Vintage year.

MUST: Grape juice or crushed grapes before fermentation.

NÉGOCIANT (France): A wine merchant or shipper who buys from different growers, packages and sells wine.

NOSE: The aroma or bouquet of a wine.

OIDIUM: Fungus disease.

OXIDATION: The generally bad effect of wine mixing with air.

PÉTILLANT (France): A light sparkle or tingle in a wine.

PHYLLOXERA: A wine disease caused by the louse *Phylloxera vastatrix*.

PRÄDIKAT (Germany): Special attribute.

PRESS WINE: The wine extracted by pressing the marc after the free run – very tannic.

PROPRIÉTAIRE (France): Owner.

QUALITÄTSWEIN (Germany): Quality wine.

QUALITÄTSWEIN MIT PRÄDIKAT (QmP) (Germany): The highest general category of German wine, Kabinett, Auslese, etc. Must be made without sugar.

RACKING: Drawing off wine from one barrel to another, leaving behind the sediment or lees.

RÉCOLTE (France): Harvest.

ROTWEIN (Germany): Red wine.

SEC (France): Dry.

SEDIMENT: The accumulation of solids, dead yeasts, etc., at the bottom of a bottle, especially in old reds. Normally a sign of

quality, common in organic wines.
SEKT (Germany): Sparkler.
SPÄTLESE (Germany): Late harvested, the fourth highest in the QmP class.
SÜSSRESERVE (Germany): Unfermented grape must added to wine before bottling to add sweetness and flavour.
TAFELWEIN (Germany): Table wine, below Qualitätswein in standard.
TANNIN: The astringent, mouth-puckering element in red wine; it softens with age and adds character.
TARTARIC ACID: Found naturally in grape juice, it can cause crystals to appear after bottling; these are harmless.
TIRAGE (France): A bottling.
TROCKEN (Germany): Dry.
TROCKENBEERENAUSLESE (Germany): Selected grapes with noble rot, top in the QmP class.
VARIETAL: A wine that takes its name from the grape it is made from.
VINTAGE: The annual grape harvest and resulting wine.
WEINGUT (Germany): A wine estate, only used by wine-makers who grow their own grapes.
WEISSHERBST (Germany): Rosé wine.
YEAST: Organisms which cause fermentation, turning grape juice into wine. Wild yeasts can spoil wine.

SELECT BIBLIOGRAPHY

A great and growing evil, the medical consequences of alcohol abuse. 1987.
BENSON, David: Why Organic Farming?
BIOLOGICAL control of insects, pests and weeds. 1964.
CARSON, Rachel: Silent Spring. 1963.
COOK, Roy: Vines and Wines Organically.
DALLAS, Philip: Italian Wines. 1983.
DAVID, Elizabeth: An Omelette and a Glass of Wine. 1984.
DAVIS, Adelle: Let's have Healthy Children. 1981.
FOOD Additives and the Consumer. 1980.
GEAR, Alan: The New Organic Food Guide. 1987.
HALLGARTEN, Fritz: Wine Scandal. 1986.
HANSSEN, Maurice: E for Additives. 1984.
HILLS, Hilda Cherry: Living Dangerously. 1973.
HILLS, Lawrence D.: Fertility without Fertilisers. 1968.
HILLS, Lawrence D.: Organic Gardening. 1977.
JACKSON, David: Grape Growing and Wine Making. 1981.
JOHNSON, Hugh: Hugh Johnson's Wine Companion. 1983.
JOHNSON, Hugh: World Atlas of Wine. 1971.
KAY, Billy and MACLEAN, Cailean: Knee Deep in Claret. 1983.
LANGENBACH, Alfred: German Wines and Vines. 1962.
McGEE: Harold: On Food and Cooking. 1986.
MacQUITTY, Jane: Pocket Guide to Champagne and Sparkling Wines. 1986.
MELLANBY, Kenneth: Pesticides and Pollution. 1970.
OGDEN, Samuel: Organic Vegetable Growing.
ORDISH, George: Biological Methods in Crop Pest Control. 1967.
PARKER, Robert: Bordeaux. 1986.
PENNING-ROWSELL, Edmund: The Wines of Bordeaux. 1979.
RAY, Cyril: The Wines of France. 1976.
ROBINSON, Jancis: Vines, Grapes and Wines. 1986.
SOIL Association Organic Husbandry: Qualifying Standards. 1983.
SUTCLIFFE Serena: Pocket Guide to the Wines of Burgundy. 1986.
TANNAHILL, Raey: Food in History. 1973.

INDEX

Abbèle, Raymond, 92
Achard-Vincent, 44, 122
Aestivalis, 178
Agriculture, Ministry of, 11, 46
Akadana, 184
Albaric ACC, 103
Albaric, Alain et Hoirie, 103, 110
Alcohol, Tobacco and Firearms, Bureau of, (BAFT), 176
Aldrin, 18
Algeria, 33
Alsace, 36-39, 58, 61-65
Amoreau, Robert, 72
André, P., 122
Anjou, 33, 96, 97
Antier, Henri et Fils, 99
Appellation Contrôleé or Appellation d'Origine Contrôleé, (AC / AOC), 60
Ardinat, José, 93
Arnaud, Germain, 109
Arzheimer Seligmacher, 154
Associazione Suolo e Salute, 161
Australia, 32-36, 58, 183
  Wine Labelling Laws, 11
Austria, 36, 37, 41, 175
  Diethylene Glycol Scandal, 50-52, 55
Auxerrois Blanc, see Pinot Noir
Avalon, 171

Baden, 137-142
Bahlinger Silverberg, 138
Ballrechter Castelberg, 139
Ballue, Guy, 68, 77
Bardolino Chiaretto. DOC, 161
Barjou, Pierre, 113
Barolo, 34, 58
Barron, P., 73
Barsac, 37, 67
Beaufort, André et Jacques, 94
Beaujolais, 31, 33, 82, 83
Beaujolais Régnie AC, Beaujolais Villages, 83
Beaumes de Venise, 36, 121
Beaune, 80
Beaune – Clos des Mariages AC, 84
Beaune – Premier Cru. AC, 84
Becker, Dr, 146, 149, 152
Begot, Mme A., 126
Beirieu, Jean-Claude, 44, 103
Belaid, Gérard, 82
Bereich Bernkastel, 142
Bergerac, 102
Berjon, Paul, 72
Bianco Toscano-Casina di Cornia. Vino da Tavola, 161

Bickensohler Steinfelsen, 139
Bickensohler Vulkanfelsaen, 140
Biokreis, 27, 137
Bioland, 27, 137
de Biso, 132
Bissa, Ernest, 109
Blanc Côteaux du Layon AC, 97
Blanc Côteaux du Village Faye AC, 97
Blanchard, Jacques et Dany, 132
Blanquette de Limoux, 44, 103, 104
Bochinger Rosenkranz, 154
Bondagon. Vin de Table, 131
Bondurand, Arlette et Lucien, 108
Bordeaux, 31-33, 37, 58, 66-79, 81
Bossard, Guy, 99
Bouchardon. Vin de Table, 104
Bouchardon, S.N.C., 104
Bouillaut, L. et Fils, 98
Bourasson. Vin de Table, 68
Bourgogne, 82
Bourgogne AC, 84-86
Bourgogne Aligote, 82
Bourgogne Aligote AC, 87
Bourgogne Passetoutgrain AC, 88
Bourgueil, 96, 97
Bourguiniana, 178
Bouron, Paul et Fils, 70
Breiling, Fritz, 155, 157, 158
Briedeler Herzchen, 142
Briedeler Nonnengarten, 143
British Industrial Research Association, 51
Brohl, Frank, 143, 144
Brunello, 34, 159
Brunet, Georges, 106
Bully Hill Vineyards, 40
Bundeserband Ökologischer Weinbau, 27, 137
Burgundy, 34-36, 58, 80-93
Burkheimer Feurberg, 140

Cabanis, Jean-Paul, 117
Cabernet d'Anjou AC, 98
Cahors, 102
California, 32, 33, 35-37, 42, 58, 178
California Certified Organic Farmers, 179
Carbardes. VDQS, 104
Carbonnel, Richard, 109
Carignan, 32, 33, 102
Cartier, Nicolas, 116
Cave Co-op, 124
Cave La Vigneronne, 124
Cêpage Grolleau Gris AC, 98
Chablis, 35, 80, 82

207

THE ORGANIC WINE GUIDE

Champagne, 34, 35, 44, 58, 59, 92-95
Chaptalisation, 29, 34, 48, 82, 159
Charbonnier, Claude, 131
Chardonnay. Vin de Pays d'Oc, 105
Chassagne-Montrachet, 81
Chasselas, 62
Château Ballue Mondon, Bordeaux AC, 68
Château Barrail des Graves, Saint Émilion AC, 68
Château Bossuet, Bordeaux Supérieur AC, 70
Château Bosqueyron, Bordeaux Supérieur AC, 70
Château Chavrignac, AC, 70
Château Chouteau, AC Saint Émilion, Grand Cru, 70
Château de Beaucastel, 121
Château de Beaucastel, AC, Châteauneuf-du-Pape, 122
Château de Boisfranc, AC, Beaujolais Supérieur, 88
Château de Prade. Bordeaux Supérieur Côtes de Castillon AC, 70
Château des Hautes Combe, Bordeaux AC, 71
Château du Moulin de Peyronin. Bordeaux AC, 72
Château du Puy. Bordeaux Supérieur AC, 72
Château Grillet, 38
Château Haut-Brion, 67
Château Jacques Blanc. St Émilion Grand Cru AC, 72
Château La Mirandole, AC, Premières Côtes de Blaye, 72
Château Le Barradis AC, Mombazillac and Bergerac, 105
Château Les Jésuites. Bordeaux AC, 73
Château Méric. Graves AC, 73
Château Moulin de Romage. Bordeaux AC, 74
Château Petit Roc. Bordeaux AC, 75
Château Petrus, 33
Château Renaissance. Bordeaux AC, 77
Château Saint-Hilaire. Graves AC, 77
Château Ste Anne, AC, Côtes de Provence, AC Bandol, 106
Château Vignelaure. VDQS Coteaux d'Aix en Provence, 106
Châteauneuf-du-Pape, 33, 120-122
Chaumont, André, 84, 90
Chaumont, Guy, 84, 91
Chemical Fertilizers, 16
Chemical Pesticides, 14, 17-19
Chenin Blanc, 35, 96
Chevelsward, 172
Chianti, 34

Chianti Classico – Casina di Cornia. DOC, 161
Chianti Putto – San Vito. DOC, 162
Chic de Balzurie. Méthode Champenoise, 77
Chinese Wine Scandal, 50
Chinon, 96
Chouet, Pierre, 72
Cinsault, 32, 33, 102, 121
de Clairac, GFA, 107
Clairbio, 131
Clairette de Die, 36, 44, 120, 122
Claret, 31, 32, 58, 66, 81
Clinton Davies, Stanley, 17
Clos de la Pèrichère. Graves AC, 78
Clos de Vougeot, 80
Clos Grand Plantier. Bordeaux Supérieur AC, 78
Clos La Maurasse. AC Graves, 78
Clos Lauriole. Bordeaux Supérieur AC, 79
Clos Le Mas. Bordeaux Supérieur AC, 79
Clos Mireille VDQS Còte de Provence, 107
Clos Petra Rossa, AC Corse, 131
Clos Rougeard AC Samur, 98
Clos St Martin. Vins de Table, 132
Co-op Vinicole de Nyonsais, 125
Coca-Cola Company, 40
Combe, Daniel, 125, 131
Concords, 178
Condrieu, 38, 120
Connesin, Père et Fils, 114
Consumer Association, 11
Cook, Roy and Irma, 172
Corbières, 103
Coronat, Augustin, 132
Costières du Gard, 103
Côteaux de Languedoc AC, 107
Côte de Beaune, 80
Côte de Nuit, 80
Côte d'Or, 80, 82
Côte Rôtie, 34, 119, 120
Coteaux d'Ajaccio AC, 132, 133
Côteaux de la Cité de Carcassonne. Vin de Pays, 107
Côteaux du Layon, 35
Côteaux du Layon-moelleux, 98
Côteaux du Tricastin, 121
Côteaux du Tricastin AC, 124
Côteaux de Beaune AC, 89
Cotes de Rhône, 33
Côtes de Toul. Vins de Table, 132
Côtes de Ventoux, 33
Côtes du Rhône, 120, 121
Côtes du Rhône. Village AC, 126
Côtes du Rhône AC, 124-126

INDEX

Côtes du Roussillon Villages, 103
Côtes de Ventoux, 121
Côtes du Vivarais, 121
Couderc, Simone, 107
Courtilleau, Émile, 102
Courtois, Claude, 114
Crêmant de Bourgogne, AC, 89
Cros, Guy, 115, 117
Crozes-Hermitage, 34, 120, 126
Cru Bourgeois, 67
Cru des Valades-Cantégrel, AC Bergerac, 107
Cru Grand Bourgeois, 67
Cru Grand Bourgeois Exceptionnel, 67
Cuvée de la Boissière. Vin Champagnisé, 132

Daltry, Ruth, 172
Daumas SCA, 129
Dauny, Nicole et Christien, 100
Deidesheimer Hofstuck, 155
Deinheimer Peterhof, 146, 147
Deinheimer Tafelstein, 149
Delacroix, Michel, 126
Delawares, 178
Delfarge-Garcia, 71
Demeter, 27, 61, 137
Denominazione di Origine Controllata, 161
Denominazione di Origine Controllata Garantita, 161
Depport, 112
Déscrambes, Gérard, 68, 77
Destand, Claude, 115
Devert, Jean-Luc, 68
Diedesfelder Rebstockel, 155
Dieudonné, Claude, 110
Dirrbach, M., 103
Doat, Thierry, 88
Domaine de Clairac. Vin de Pays de l'Hérault, 107
Domaine de Gressac. Vin de Pays des Côteaux de Cèze, 108
Domaine de la Chaume. VDQS Côteaux de Pierrevert, 108
Domaine de la Gautière. Vin de Pays des Côteaux des Baronnies, 109
Domaine de Landue. AC Côtes de Provence, 109
Domaine de l'Eau Salée. Vin de Table, 109
Domaine de l'Île. AC Limoux, Vins de Pays de l'Aude, 109, 110
Domaine de l'Île des Sables. Vin de Table, 110
Domaine de Malaric. Vin de Pays de l'Uzège, 110
Domaine de Mallaval, AC Beaujolais Villages, 89

Domaine de Réguse. VDQS Côtes de Pierrevert, 110
Domaine de St Crescent. VDQS Corbières, 110
Domaine de Snhilac. Vin de Pays du Gard, 110
Domaine de Trevallon, 34, 103, 110
Domaine des Cèdres. AC Côtes du Rhône, 127
Domaine des Coccinelles. AC Côtes du Rhône, 128
Domaine des Dorices, Muscadet de Sèvres et Maine, AC, 98
Domaine des Nuets. VDQS Côtes de Provence, 111
Domaine des Palats. AC Corbières, 112
Domaine du Bas-Deffens. VDQS Côteaux Varios, 113
Domaine du Bois Noir. AC Cotes du Rhône, 127
Domaine du Fumat, 113
Domaine Gendre Marsalet. AC Côtes de Bergerac, 113
Domaine Grand Bourry. VDQS Costière de Gard, 114
Domaine Les Cardelines. AC Côtes du Rhône, 127
Domaine Martini. AC Côteaux d'Ajaccio, 132
Domaine Richaud. AC Côtes du Rhône and Côtes du Rhône Villages, 129
Domaine Richeaume. AC Côtes de Provence, 114
Domaine St André de Figuière. AC Côtes and VDQS, 114
Domaine St Cyriaque. Vins de Pays and VDQS, 114
Domaine Saint-Apollinaire. AC Côtes du Rhône, 129
Dopff et Irion, 62
Doub, Michael, 141
Drighi, Roberto, 162
Duchess, 178
Durkheimer Feurberg, 155
Durrbach, Éloi et Jacqueline, 111
Dutheil de la Rochère, François, 106
Duttenhofer, Franz-Joseph, 147, 149
Dynorga. Vin de Table, 129

Échezaux, 80
Edelzwicker, 37, 62
Edenkobener Heidengartn, 155
EEC,
    Farming Produce Control Regulations, 17
    Labelling Regulations, 39, 41, 46
    Water Safety Limits, 18
    Wine Regulations, 47, 61, 170
Elvira, 178

England, 36, 170-174
Ensheimer Kochelberg, 150
Estève, Jean-Pierre, 126
Étienne, Jean-Marc, 112, 113
European Economic Community, 11
Exploitations Dubost, 70
Eymann, Rudolf, 155, 156

Fabré, René, 128
Falerian, 43
Falleri, Jean-Claude, 114
Faust, Serge, 94
Fédération Européene des Syndicats d'Agrobiologistes, 21
Flonheimer Pfaffenburg, 150
Fontant, Duccio, 161, 164
Foucault, Ch. et F., 98
Four Chimneys Farm Winery, 180
Fournier, Isnel, 70
France, 32, 33, 38, 39, 58-133
Franscisci, François, 131
Fransoret, Roger, 94
Frascati, 38
Freulon, Yves, 96-98
Frick, Pierre et Fils, 63
Fugazza Sisters, 162

Gaillac, 102
Garonne, 58
Garrey, Hubert, 91
Gattinara, 34
de la Gautière, 109
Georget, Christian, 97
Germany, 36-39, 58, 134-158
Gigondas, 33, 121
Giraudet, Louis, 110
Givry, 81
Gonnheimer Mandelgarten, 156
Gonnheimer Martinshohe, 156
Gonnheimer Sonnenberg, 156
Goujot, Michel, 132
Grange Hermitage, 34
Grape Varieties, 31-38
Graves, 32, 67
Grenouilles, 82
Grunerner Altenberg, 140
Guérin, Gabriel, 78
Guillot, Alain, Janine et Pierre, 85, 88, 90
Guintrand, Jean-Pierre, 126
Guiraud, Jean, 107
Guldentaler Apostelberg, 145
Guldentaler Schlossekapelle, 145
Guntersblumer Bornpfad, 150
Gunersblumer Eiserne Hand, 151
Guntersblumer Himmeltal, 151
Guntersblumer Steig Terr, 151
Guntersblumer Vogelsgarten, 151
Gutturnio dei Colli Piacentini, 162

Haraszthy, Agostan, 178
Hauck, Walter, 150
Hautes Côtes de Beaune AC, 90
Hawkins, Charles, 177
d'Heilly, Pierre, 88
Hérail, Mme Edmond, 110
zu Herrnsheim, Freiherr Heyl, 153
Hoesch, Henning, 114
Huberdeau, Martine, 88
Hungary, 37
Hussent, Thomas, 94

Ihringer Fohrenberg, 141
Institut National des Appellations d'Origine des Vins et Eaux-de-Vie, 60
International Federation of Organic Agricultural Movements, 168, 170
Italy, 34, 37, 38, 58, 159-166
  Methyl Alcohol Scandal, 50, 53-55
  Wine Regulations, 160, 161
Jalifier, Jacques, 124
Japan, 184
  Import Duties, 185
  Labelling Regulations, 53
  Wine Scandal, 52, 53
Javillier, Jean, 86, 87, 91, 92
Jouannin-Cormier, 108
Jougla, L.C., 119

Klevner, see Pinot Noir
Knodel, Konrad, 145
Kopfer, Weingut, 139, 140
Krover Paradies, 143

La Beylie. Bordeaux AC, 68
La Tache, 80
La Vieille Ferme, 121
La Vieille Ferme. AC Côtes de Ventoux, 130
Labelling, 11, 39-42, 49, 176, 177, 183
Labudde, Klaus, 138-141
Lagoutte, Jean-Paul, 83
Landwein der Mosel , 143
Languedoc, 32, 33
Laufener Altenberg, 141
Laval, Georges, 94
Le Clos des Grives. AC Côtes du Jura, 131
Le Corton, 80
Le Maire Boucher, 21, 27, 61
Le Montrachet, 82
Leroux, Gérard, 101
Les Clos, 82
Letuvée, Paul, 94
Liebfraumilch, 36, 134, 146
Limoux, 44
Lindquist, Robert, 40
Lirac, 33, 121
Listel, 105

INDEX

Listel – rouge Roubis, Vin de Table, 115
Litenis. Vin de Table, 115
Loire, 37, 58, 95-102
Longworth, Nicholas, 178
Lonsheimer Schonbert, 151
Lou Canterio. Vin de Pays de l'Hérault, 115
Loupia, Jean-Claude et Annie, 21, 26, 104, 107
Luberon, 121
Lucmaret, Guy, 73
Ludwigshoher Teufelskopf, 152
Luginbuhl, Antoine, 161, 164

Mâcon AC, 90
Magnieval, Frères, 78
Maikammerer Heiligenberg, 157
Maikammerer Mandelhohe, 157
de Malaric, 110, 117
Martini – Ledentu, 132, 133
Marzolph, Wolfgang, 154, 158
Mas de Gourgonnier. AC Côteaux d'Aix en Provence Les Baux, 116
Mas des Garrigues. Vins de Table, 132
Mas Madagascar. Vin de Pays du Gard, 117
Mathieu, Georges, 120
Maugey, René, 70
Mauros, Jean-François, 78
Médoc, 32, 34, 67
Mercurey, 81, 90, 91
Merdinger Buhl, 141
Messerschmitt, Gg., 154
Mettenheimer, 152
Mettenheimer Goldberg, 152
Mettenheimer Schlossberg, 153
Meursault, 80
Meursault AC, 91
Meyer, Eugene, 63
Michelin, Noël, 21, 22, 118
Midi and the South West, 62, 102-118
Millet, Marcel, 126
Minervois, 103, 117
Monbazillac, 102
Monbouche, René, 113
Mondavi, Robert, 37
Montagny, 81
Montrachet, 35
Mornai, Jacques-Victor, 105, 118
Morocco, 33
Moscateo Bianco, 36
Mosel-Saar-Ruwer, 142-145
Moselblümchen, 142
Moselle, 58
Moulin à Vent, 33, 81
Mourvèdre, 102, 121
Muller Thurgau, 31, 36, 142, 146, 154
Muscadelle, 67
Muscadet, 36, 96, 99

Muscat de Beaumes de Venise-La-Vieille Ferme AC, 129
Musso, Jean, 90

Nahe, 145-146
Nature et Progrès, 27, 61
Naturland, 27, 137
Nebbiolo, 34
Neustadter Grain, 158
New Zealand, 31, 36
Niersteiner, 146
Niersteiner Brudersberg, 153
Niersteiner Kranzberg, 153
Nouteau-Cérisier, J., 97, 98, 100
Nuits St Georges, 80

Oinos, 27, 137
Organic Agriculture, 13, 15, 17, 20, 21, 27
Organic Viticulture, 12, 17
Organic Wine, 13-21, 56, 61
Orvieto, 38
Ott, Henri, 107

Pedicino, S. and C., 164
Pefchlow, Anne, 141
Penedes, 167
Penning-Rowsell, Edmund, 175
Pepys, Samuel, 66
Pérignon, Dom Pierre, 44, 92
Perrin, Jean-Pierre, 121
Perrin, M., 129, 130
Perrin, Ste Ferme des Vignobles, 122
Pfalzer Landwein, 158
Phylloxera vastatrix, 15, 59, 136, 137, 177, 178, 179
Piemonte, 54
Piesporter Michelsberg, 142
Pinard, Georges et Guy, 133
Pineau des Charentes, 132, 133
Piroux, Alain, 74
Planiol, Robert, 132
Platière, René Bosse, 83
Poggio Alle Rocche. Vino da Tavola, 164
Poirrier, Viviane et Régis, 94
Pomerol, 33
Pons, Dominique, 127
Pouilly Fumé, 37, 95
Pouilly-Fuisse, 81
Pouizin, Paulette, 126
Provence, 21, 33, 59, 103
Puligny-Montrachet, 80
Puligny-Montrachet AC, 91
Punedericher Marienburg, 144

Quotidianus. Vin de Table, 117
Qupé, 40

Rampon, André, 83
Rateau, Pierrette et Jean-Claude, 84, 89, 91
Reiler Goldlay, 144
Reiler Mullay-Hofberg, 144
Reiler vom heissen Stein, 144
Reserve St Christophe, 117
Rheinhessen, 146-153
Rheinpfalz, 153-158
Rhône, 33, 38, 44, 58, 119
Richard, Jean-Paul, 68, 75
Richaud, Marcel, 129
Rioja, 33, 35, 58, 167
Riparia, 178
Rizzardi, Antonio, 161, 165, 166
Rogerie, Michel, 70, 79
Romanée-Conti, 80
Rosé d'Anjou AC, 100
Rosso di Castellina. Vino da Tavola, 164
Rousillon, 32, 33
Ruffin, Yves, 95
Rully, 81
Rupestris, 178
Russia, 53

St Christophe, 133
Saint Émilion, 32, 6l7
St Joseph, 34
Saint-Véran, 81
Sake, 184
Sancerre, 34, 37, 95
Sancerre AC, 100
Sander, Otto Heinrich, 152, 153
Saumur, 35, 96
Saumur AC, 101, 102
Sauterne, 37, 67
Savigny-Les-Beaunes, 80
Schmidd-Labudde, Gerda, 138-141
Schnell, Dr Heinrich, 150-152
Scoonmaker, Frank, 142
Schuhmacher, Kai, 141
Sedlescrombe Vineyard, 172, 187
Sélection des Grains Nobles, 62
Serra, Father Junipero, 178
Sessacq, R., 78
Sircana, A. and L., 164
Soave Classico. DOC, 165
Soil Association, 27, 170
la Solana, 104
South Africa, 31, 33, 134
Spain, 35, 58, 167-169
Sparham, Tim, 112

Steffens, Harald, 142-144
Stenz, André, 64
Suole e Salute, 37
Switzerland, 175

Tavel, 212
Tavel Rosé, 33
Taylor, Walter, 40
Terre et Océan, 27, 61
Terre et Vie, 21, 27, 61
Terres Blanches. AC Côteaux d'Aix en Provence Les Baux, 119
Tokay, 39
Tokay d'Alsace, 62
Tomalin, Nicholas, 55
Touraine, 33, 96
Trarbacher Scholossberg, 144
Trautwein, Hans-Peter, 138
Tripp, Dr H. R. Howard, 171
Trollinger, 36

UK Food Labelling Regulations ,41
United States National Academy of Sciences, 18
USA, 176
  Wine Additive Regualtions, 48
  Wine Labelling Laws, 11, 176, 177

Valdepenas, 167, 168
Valpolicella – Classico Superiore. DOC, 166
Verdet, Alain, 86, 87, 89
Vernaccia de San Gimignano. DOC, 166
Vida Sana, 27, 168
Vignobles de la Jasse. AC Côtes du Rhône, 131
Vin de Table -Jougla, 118
Volnay Santenots AC, 92
Voss, Roger, 175
Vouvray, 35, 96

Werner, Gebr, 150, 151
Wick, Udo, 143
Windesheimer Rosenberg, 145
Wollemesheimer Mutterle, 158
World Health Authority, 45
Wurtz-Sigrist, Richard, 65

Zeller Kreuzberg, 158
Zellertal, Churpfalz-Keller, 154, 158
Zinfandel, 35, 179

Reader's Report Form for *The Organic Wine Guide*

Wine merchants, shops and restaurants not already included in the guide.

Name: ....

Address: ....

....

....

Telephone number: ....

Comments: ....

....

....

....

....

Your comments on existing stockists – their ranges, their information on organic wine, etc.:

....

....

....

....

IN BLOCK LETTERS PLEASE:

Name: ....

Address : ....

....

....

Please send to: Charlotte Mitchell, Real Foods, Ashley Place, Edinburgh EH6 5PX. *Thank You*

Report on organic wines not included in
The Organic Wine Guide

Please send information if you are an organic wine producer or if you know of one, to enable us to update fully this guide.

Name ....

Address: ....

....

....

Telephone number: ....

Wines produced: ....

....

....

....

....

Certification :

....

....

....

....

Any other relevant information :

....

....

....

....

Please send to: Charlotte Mitchell, Real Foods, Ashley Place, Edinburgh EH6 5PX. *Thank You*